Nonpublic School Aid

The Law, Economics, and Politics of American Education

E. G. West
Carleton University

Lexington Books
D.C. Heath and Company
Lexington, Massachusetts
Toronto   London

Library of Congress Cataloging in Publication Data

Main entry under title:

Nonpublic school aid.

   Includes index.
   1. State aid to private schools—United States—Addresses, es-
says, lectures. I. West, E.G.
KF4220.A75N65   379'.322'0973   75-31289
ISBN 0-669-00337-9

Second printing, May 1977.

Published simultaneously in Canada.

Printed in the United States of America.

International Standard Book Number: 0-669-00337-9

Library of Congress Catalog Card Number: 75-31289

Contents

Foreword

Seldom do scholars capture the attention of their peers the way E.G. West did with the seminal essay in this volume. Professor West brought the essay with him to a small gathering of scholars who met in Chicago a year ago to explore new directions for research on contemporary issues of educational freedom. No sooner had he introduced his ideas than fellow conferees started probing for more details, until finally he found himself presenting the entire essay and leading a lively discussion of one point after another. At the conclusion of this spirited session, there was unanimous agreement that the essay be introduced to a wider audience of scholars concerned with the financing of education.

The Center for Independent Education, which had arranged the conference to help guide the educational programs of the Liberty Fund and the Institute for Humane Studies, took the initiative by inviting several experts in the fields of law, economics, and education to prepare formal critiques of the essay. Their eagerness to do so confirmed our expectations that the work would stimulate constructive debate among scholarly critics. Their comments were appreciative and forthright, as were Professor West's responses to them.

The result of this exchange is presented here in a volume that contains perhaps the most advanced analysis and solution of the "school aid" problem offered to date.

Benjamin A. Rogge
Conference Chairman

October 1, 1975
Wabash College

Preface

This book is about the present financial difficulty of nonpublic schools in America. It inquires about the role, positive or negative, that government can play, does play, or ought to play. The opening essay sets the problem in the context of recent Supreme Court verdicts on government attempts in the 1970s to aid impecunious parochial schools. This essay, the first draft of which I completed in 1974 during a sabbatical leave at the Law Department, University of California at Berkeley, was originally intended as an independent piece; indeed, one version of it is scheduled to appear in a 1976 issue of *The Journal of Law and Economics*. Wider attention and interest were kindled after an incidental and brief verbal description of the argument at a conference sponsored by the Centre for Independent Education in Chicago in October 1974. The convener, George Pearson, urged that a reaction to the work be gathered from eight various specialists in the fields of law, economics, and education.

The final stage in the evolution of the book was reached when Mike McCarroll, the director of Lexington Books, made the intriguing proposal that I write a reply to each individual commentary and at similar length. Speaking for myself, this turned out to be a happy suggestion. The replies that I was prodded to write (also included herein) gave me much greater scope to develop my initial theme, and often in unexpected ways. The result is a book whose novel format resembles somewhat the structure of the medieval disputation! Whatever the final strengths or weaknesses in my now fully elaborated argument, I have benefited substantially and in a constructive and creative way from all the other contributions; indeed my second essay in this book, *The Philosophic and Historic Interpretation of the First Amendment*, would not have been written without their instigation.

Acknowledgments are due: to *The Childhood and Government Program*, University of California at Berkeley (where I met many stimulating colleagues in the fields of law and economics); to George Pearson and The Center For Independent Education for the initiative and considerable help in launching the book; Mike McCarroll of Lexington Books for suggesting its final shape; and finally to my wife Ann who, as usual, has provided indispensible editorial and typing work.

List of Contributors

James M. Buchanan
Virginia Polytechnic Institute
  and State University
Department of Economics

John E. Coons
University of California
  at Berkeley
School of Law

Donald A. Erickson
Simon Fraser University
Department of Education

Roger A. Freeman
Senior Fellow
Hoover Institution

Milton Friedman
University of Chicago
Department of Economics

James D. Koerner
Program Officer
Alfred P. Sloan Foundation

Murray N. Rothbard
Polytechnic Institute of New York
Department of Economics

Stephen D. Sugarman
University of California
  at Berkeley
School of Law

An Economic Analysis of the Law and Politics of Nonpublic School "Aid"

E.G. West

The current legal controversy on nonpublic school (or parochial) aid makes much economics literature on the reform of public school finance seem rather "academic." The arguments of economists for education vouchers, in particular, appear seriously incomplete because of inadequate recognition of constitutional constraints. Of American private schools 90 percent are church-related. The First Amendment problem must clearly be confronted if a voucher scheme is to be seriously entertained. This essay is written in the belief that economists can contribute to the legal debate and in the hope that this will help to clear the way for serious consideration of voucher and other schemes based on their merits.

Recent Supreme Court judgment has been based on much implicit economic reasoning; yet, as will be argued here, most of it is not consistent with current economic analysis. My first basic point stems from conventional economic writing which treats education as generating "two separate products." The first is the private family benefit. The second consists of alleged public benefits in the form of "externalities" that can be internalized through public financing. The economic model that applies, it seems, is therefore that of joint supply. This reasoning, however, involves no inherent reference to "subsidy" or "aid." Consider the classic illustration of joint supply in economic literature, the case of the beef and hides. This literature does not argue that because neither beef nor hides can be produced without the other, the beef purchaser is *subsidizing* the hides purchaser (or vice versa). Since education matches this joint supply situation, as I shall argue, the concept of subsidy is likewise inappropriate. This reasoning has important implications for legal questions of whether particular state actions are unconstitutional because they involve "aid" (i.e., subsidy) to parochial schools.

My second basic economic argument stems from evidence (to be quoted) showing that families in *all* income groups pay substantial sums in education taxes, especially when considered over their lifetime. Suppose

This paper was made possible by research facilities provided by the University of California, School of Law, Childhood and Government Project, between January and August 1974. I would like to acknowledge valuable discussion with: Norton Grubb, F. Raymond Marks, Stephen Sugerman, Robert Mnookin, David Kirp, James Moody, Gary Hoachlander, John McManus, and Michael Bordo. The paper has also benefited from discussion with André Daniere, Institute of Human Sciences, Boston College.

1

some of or all these sums were collected as "user taxes" at the door of the school instead of indirectly, as at present. These user taxes could replace either the existing taxes on families who use the school system or the lifetime expected taxes. In the latter case, one would require a loan scheme for lower education. Suppose, too, that these charges are viewed predominantly as paying for private family benefits from education. The constitutional "problem" would then be seen from a considerably different perspective. This would follow because first, the proportion of finance viewed as "aid" from the "government" would be drastically reduced, and second, imposing user tax charges on ("parochial") nonusers of the public schools—so that they pay twice for nonpublic schooling—would indeed be seen as infringing on the Free Exercise clause.

My third economic argument develops from the second. It predicts a reformed financing system that would enable those state governments that now desire marginally to ease the financial problems of parochial schools, to do so without facing the present legal obstacles. This third argument has force and relevance whether or not the first (joint supply) argument is accepted. It will be elaborated in the section entitled "Resolution of the Problem."

On the legal side, the basic issue is the Supreme Court's search for a coherent interpretation of the First Amendment. Intentionally or not, that amendment seems ambiguous to some. There are *two* religious clauses. The first states that "Congress shall make no law, respecting an establishment of religion." The second states that Congress shall make no law "prohibiting the free exercise thereof." Recent legal discussion has produced at least three conflicting interpretations.[1] First, the strict "separationists," such as Leo Pfeffer,[2] believe that there should be no aid to religious schools in any degree or form. Second, "cooperationists" such as Robert Drinan[3] argue that the state should offer some cooperation with nonpublic religious schools because otherwise the state would be giving aid exclusively to the teaching of antireligion or "nonbelief"; it would thus fail in its duty to be impartial. The third view is that of the "neutralists." Neutrality is defined either in the sense of Professor Kurland's[4] "religion blindness" in policy operations or in the sense of Professor Katz's[5] appropriate religious freedom so as to prevent public schooling from "silently teaching the unimportance of religion."

The separationists place primary emphasis on the Establishment clause. Respect for the Free Exercise clause, they believe, follows automatically. The cooperationists, in contrast, give most weight to the Free Exercise clause. They contend that the Establishment clause is only invoked if the state attempts aid to sectarian schools in addition to providing adequate religious education in public schools. The neutrality advocates, on the other hand, attempt something like an equal balancing, fusion, or merger of the two religious clauses.

I shall discuss several decisions related to recent state government attempts to relieve parochial schools, but shall concentrate especially on the *Nyquist* case decided on June 25, 1973.[6] The first part of the essay reviews the economist's usual "tools of the trade" concerning "optimal" subsidies to education. The second part critically applies this analysis to the details of *Nyquist*. The third part, on positive economics, suggests one previously untried policy that could be acceptable to all parties in the New York case.

Educational Public Goods and Optimal Subsidies

In economics the two most quoted normative reasons for state intervention in education are: first, the protection of children against negligent parents, and second, the encouragement of beneficial "externalities." The first is generally regarded as being met by compulsory education laws.[7] The externalities argument, which will receive more attention here, is based on the assumption that persons outside the family unit receive benefits from each child's education.[8] It will be argued in this article, however, that there is a third reason for intervention, one that is especially pertinent to the legal controversy. The tax system is used to enable people to buy their own education from their lifetime incomes (like an installment system). This argument will emerge gradually from an analysis of externalities and in the context of religious clauses.

Under the externalities rubric, each family's utility function includes as an argument the consumption of education by *other* families. It is *assumed* in several models that each family has a nonzero marginal rate of substitution between another family's consumption of education and each good it consumes itself (including its own child's education). This conventional analysis then concludes that, for economic optimality, these marginal rates of substitution in consumption, summed over all families, must be equal to the societal marginal rate of transformation in production.

To be completely persuasive, the externality argument needs the support of evidence that externalities really exist and are positive at the margin. Since the evidence is usually absent, most writers resort to explicit or implicit judgment that positive external benefits exist. To get my own analysis started, I shall initially accept this conventional approach, not because of any personal preference, but because the Supreme Court's arguments seem to assume it.

When external benefits occur, the "production" of schooling for child j can be described in terms of joint supply of output; a unit of education simultaneously satisfies both private and community demands. The optimal solution in the usual literature is to extend consumption until the vertical sum of the demand prices, shown as ΣD in Figure 1, is equal to marginal cost *MC*. This ΣD curve (line) is obtained by vertically adding all points on the D_j and D_k curves (lines). The D_k curve represents the demand, not of a single neighbor but of all neighbors collectively. Aggregate demand ΣD cuts the supply (*MC*) curve at *G* giving an optimal consumption of Q_2. The two separate demand prices at this comsumption are, respectively, P_c (the price to the community) and P_f (the price to the family). The sum of these two prices just equals the total per-unit cost of providing the education service ($P_c + P_f = OB$). If, on the other hand, the parties were to act independently, they would each adjust until their *separate* marginal evaluations would equal marginal cost. In this case family *j* would purchase only *OM* education. At this position the aggregate evaluation would be higher than marginal cost by *HE = MK*. Thus, coordinated, nonindependent action is optimal.

I shall now extend this analysis in terms of a stylized community, the abstract features or assumptions of which will be relaxed later. It is a community of 20 people consisting of four unmarried adults, four married pairs of adults with one child each, and four older adults who are childless or whose children have grown up. Suppose that both the preferences (or tastes) for its own child's education and the income of each family with a child are identical, and are represented by demand curve D_j. Suppose also that all preferences to internalize the external benefits from other families' children's education are also identical and positive. *Since it is most quoted in the literature,* I shall *assume* that the main external benefit is the greater freedom from property crime as a result of education. (I do not commit myself to this particular judgment.)

I shall assume a voluntary establishment of some sort of educational external benefits "club," because in this small numbers case there is a greater incentive for each individual to reveal his true preferences for such benefits and the transaction costs of collection are low (i.e., the "free rider problem" is not large.) The neighbors are charged P_c with respect to each child's education. The parents pay a price of P_f at the door of the school. It is no accident that I assume a positive-priced public system. This can be "justified" here for immediate analytic purposes, but the realism of the assumption is not too strained in any case. Positive prices were a feature of the American public system a century ago, and they are still characteristic of higher education today. More importantly, I shall argue that there is a sense in which the education taxes paid by parents of all income groups constitute a charge for private benefits. On my type of analysis a zero price to parents is possible—but only by coincidence. It would occur where the D_j curve was so far to the left that *Dk* and ΣD overlap at the optimal point. For example this would be the case if D_j cut the *x*-axis at *M*, or if *MC* was below *Pf*. Notice that all parties are better off at equilibrium in my model. With identical tastes for educational benefits, each and every neighbor will

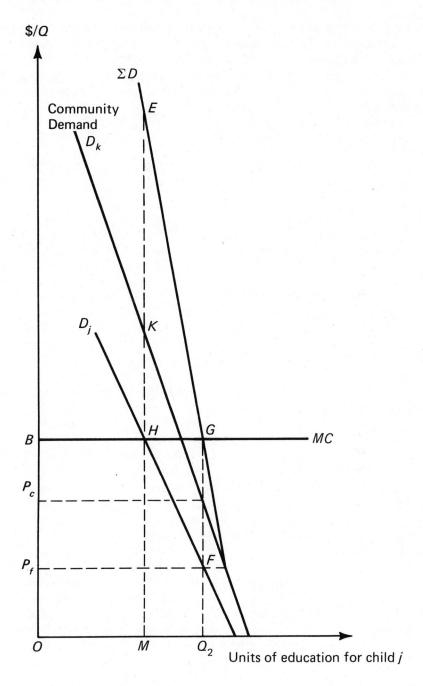

Figure 1

have equally improved his/her welfare in the sense of having made optimal investments via the tax system (or other finance schemes) to internalize external benefits.

There is nothing in theory that necessarily precludes production of 'public goods' through voluntary clubs or associations. The selection of the appropriate agency for generating public goods is a separate matter. It involves, among other things, the full nature of the 'free rider' problem, the question of minimizing transaction costs, and the geographic or other definitions of a "community." Even if public rather than private organization *is* selected, my model does not inevitably call for an elitist "state" independent of its 20 people or enjoying externally ordained finance called "public funds," a term that is much used in legal arguments. The money used by the community, or the neighbors ($P_c Q_2$ in Figure 1), could be, and presumably would be in a 'perfect democracy' voluntarily supplied by individuals in order to internalize the external benefits. The description of such money as "public funds" can be misleading. The funds originate privately and would not flow through public or private channels without taxpayer motivation to internalize the external benefits of education.

Now assume that our community of 20 people is divided evenly between the religious and the nonreligious. Assume also that no individual is hostile to a scheme of collectivized finance to internalize the external educational benefits on the grounds that it encourages religion or nonreligion. (Or, if some individuals do have such objections, the intensity of external benefits outweighs them; that is, there are positive *net* external benefits.) In the absence of any special religious clauses in the Constitution, the equilibrium solution would remain as before, even though some of the external benefits would not be purchased from religious (or nonreligious) schools. Assume, moreover, that there is nothing in the production functions of either type of school that severely changes the output ratio of external to internal benefits. An average standardized teaching hour in either school, for instance, is supposed to have identical improvements in functional literacy; since literacy is associated with crime reduction, we may regard it here as the chief surrogate for external benefits.

Next introduce a provision, similar to that of the First Amendment of the U.S. Constitution, forbidding any law to "establish" or "prohibit" religion. The strict separationists would now insist that the government's purchase of external benefits from the education of the children in the religious schools should be terminated. While the neighbors value only secular external benefits, these are jointly supplied with religious education. Since the latter will be encouraged when the community shares the cost, the Constitution will be violated, according to the separationists, and the public support to this joint production must cease. Note that believers will not exclusively bear the burden of this cessation; nonbelievers will be equally restricted in their "purchase," or internalization, of external benefits. Moreover, the continued public contributions to the cost of educating children of nonreligious families will continue to yield external benefits to the religious families (again, in the secular form of crime reduction). Note also that in making these public contributions to education, religious families in our particular model are not "paying twice" for the education of their children; they are paying for two distinct things: external benefits from the public education of the children of others (nonbelievers) and private benefits from the education of their own. They are no longer charged the "user price" P_f at the public school because they no longer use it. They continue to pay once for private benefits of education, but this time at a nonpublic school.

The neutralists will emphasize that the withdrawal of the neighbors' demand curve (D_k) from the religious sector of education will effect an increase in tuition (from P_f to OB). They will claim that this results in a discriminating burden on religious schooling. Since public schooling will become cheaper relative to religious schooling, there is, they will insist, a bias toward inculcating secularism or nonbelief. The price of nonreligious education will be reduced below that of religious education. The Establishment clause of the First Amendment, the neutralists argue, should be treated as supporting the Free Exercise clause. The above policy, just like a sumptuary tax, will weaken religious schooling. The separationists could reply, however, that the (incidental) effect of the described government intervention is not to *prohibit* exercise of religion but simply to increase its costs.

Economic reasoning can clarify most of these issues. At the level of general equilibrium analysis, a given action by government cannot help but affect various individuals and agencies in society in a variety of ways. Government action, for instance, often affects the prices of various inputs (factors), and thus affects incomes and employment via market interaction. To demand that government action be prohibited simply because it has *some* effects on the welfare of religious individuals, or of anybody else, is unrealistic. The reduction of the price of public schooling to a family that is caused by the inclusion of the neighbors' demand curve through the public sector, is merely one more example of the (Walrasian) general equilibrium, or side effects of government action. Notice that I am not arguing that the *cost* of education changes. This remains constant; I am assuming constant returns to scale. But when this *cost* remains the same at *OB*, the *share* of it between families and neighbors can alter according to public policy. Thus, the *price* to the family may fall if the neighbors offer to share in the (constant) cost of *OB*. But of course if the price falls the family will demand more.

It is very important to note that in this case the government is not *subsidizing* public school users. The neighbors' demand curve D_k is strictly for the purchase of benefits which must be had for all or for none; and are consumed *pari passu* with internal benefits. This is a joint supply situation which may be analyzed in exactly the same way as the classic example of hides and beef for their respective separate markets. At equilibrium under competitive conditions, the marginal cost of slaughtering cattle will equal the sum of the prices for beef and hides (just as in Figure 1 at Q_2, D_j *plus* D_k equals *MC*). As has been recently emphasized,[9] the socially relevant marginal cost to the purchasers of hides of servicing their demands is the marginal cost of slaughtering the cattle, *minus the market price of beef.* Similarly, the price of beef is equal to *MC minus the market price of hides.* The prevailing prices of each product will depend on the height of the demand curve for the other (jointly supplied) product. It is incorrect to describe the effect of a changing price of one product on the price of another as a subsidy. The neutralists can employ this same analysis however. If government decides to purchase secular external benefits from sectarian schools, then the resulting fall in sectarian school fees is not a subsidy. The government would not subsidize religious schooling any more than the purchasers of hides subsidize purchasers of beef.

Now consider the practicality of a government confining its "purchases" to strictly secular teaching in sectarian schools, and whether, in terms of the legal doctrine growing out of *Walz*[10] and *Nyquist,* it can, in fact, avoid becoming "excessively entangled." Basing the decision on the presence of "entanglement" would seem to the economist to be ill-advised. Joint supply in production *necessarily* involves entanglement in the sense of cost interdependency. There is no other way. But this does not, to the economist, imply economic coercion. The purchaser of beef is entangled with the purchaser of hides in the sense that both obtain their products from a common source. This, however, is not an entanglement which inhibits or coerces the market action of either party. For each set of agents, the hide purchaser and the beef purchaser, the action of the other is a parameter if we assume competition. It is exogenous. But within that fact each can alter its market behavior freely. For example, hide purchasers would be free to reduce their demand for hides, thus reducing their market price. But this act would raise the market price of beef. There is a close parallel with education. If, for instance, literacy reduces crime and Bible reading in religious schools promotes literacy, then crime reduction and religious training are jointly supplied products. A government, as purchaser of one product (literacy and therefore crime reduction), is just as fully "entangled" with the purchaser of religious instruction as is the purchaser of beef with the purchaser of hides. True, in the *Nyquist* decision the Supreme Court was sensitive to an entanglement that it describes as "excessive." But excessive entanglement is only meaningful against some standard of normal entanglement. This standard is unfortunately likely to be "considerable" entanglement, however the jurists may judge it on a case-by-case basis.

The source of the confusion to the economist is the attempt to treat *joint* supply as *separate* supply. Yet, this futile attempt is what the court requires when it demands the policing of public money in parochial schools in such a way that it does not favor the other product of education—religious indoctrination. Not surprisingly, actual attempts by state governments inherently imply "excessive" entanglement, and it is then an easy matter for the court subsequently to strike them down.

The preceding reasoning is that of an economist. Some legal experts have responded to me that a judge would accept the logic but argue that it does not satisfy the need for *symbolism* that the law requires. There are different kinds of by-products, some of them more "visible" or contiguous than others. The closer they are to each other physically (or visibly), and provided that a government is responsible for them, the more sensitive is the judicial mind to the traditional spirit of the religious clauses of the Constitution. As I understand it, this argument might be further illustrated as follows. Suppose the government made large purchases of a certain kind of timber for use in a new public housing program. Suppose that the sawing of the timber created a considerable by-product of sawdust, and of the quality which happens to be exactly right for burning incense in churches. Incense was previously a high cost factor in religion, but now its cost falls dramatically. Such a government housing product would presumably not be struck down as an aid to religion even though it has the consequence of advancing religion. Whence the difference? Public housing and incense are less "contiguous," less "visible." The by-product in education, in contrast, is more clearly connected with government activity. This being so, there is more potential for political attention and dispute. Such an answer is suggested by the Nyquist court's specially extended definition of entanglement to include an entanglement that encourages "political strife."

For those who attach importance to the above reasoning, my model suggests possible alternative government methods of financing that respect it. One way, although probably not a very practical one, would be for the government to purchase the educational output that it desired in the same way that it would purchase beef (separately from hides). It could, for instance, offer substantial financial prizes to those who could pass literacy attainment tests. Individuals would be free to buy instruction from all kinds of institutions (if necessary, with the aid of loan schemes), and these could include parochial schools. While there could be an equal by-product effect advancing religion, it is less likely to meet with juridical disapproval since the connection is more remote.

A further analysis of my earlier model will suggest a different and more practical modification. Periodic cost increases in public education could, in the future, be financed by a different sort of tax, namely a user tax, or a special price confronting the clientele of public schools exclusively. Since only users—that is, public school clientele—would face this price, patrons of nonpublic schools would begin to enjoy some relief. Indeed, the deterioration of the financial situation of their schools could cease. Under this scenario any attempt to impose charges on nonusers would be equivalent to raising special levies on sectarian minorities who do not use public railways to help pay for the rail fares of those who do. The "visibility" of this encroachment would presumably lead the Supreme Court to reject it. Notice, however, that what is visible here is the violation of the Free Exercise clause, not the Establishment clause. Presumably the court would again be sensitive to this violation on the grounds of the danger of political discord.

We must now examine more closely the justification of confronting parents with modest degrees of positive pricing for education. Return to my model of 20 people. In Figure 1, total expenditure on education at equilibrium quantity Q_2 has been described as being shared between the community which pays $BGFP_f$ and the family which pays P_fFQ_2O. This diagram, like most others in the literature (see, for example, note 8), although it is rarely made explicit, already implies positive prices to parents. Positive prices appear more plausible here because *my particular model assumes equality of incomes and tastes*. This is initially useful for heuristic purposes. Eventually such special assumptions will be relaxed. Pending this, we now make the extra assumption that each adult is the parent of one child at some time of his/her life. The combined assumptions now rule out any redistributive function of education.

More strikingly, there can now be a dramatic reduction in, or erosion of, the role of externalities. The phenomenon to be explained is the selection of OQ_2 as optimal expenditure. The existence of significant externalities plus internal benefits, the conventional explanation, is only one possible *hypothesis*. Another hypothesis can now compete with it. Consider the family presently paying the direct education fee of P_f. Does it really receive the rest of the payment of FG from others, or does it pay indirectly for most or all of this too? The adult members of this family contributed taxes before marriage; they will continue to do so after their child leaves school. It is possible in my model (with equal incomes, family sizes, etc.) that each adult *can be regarded as fully paying for his/her own child's education*, and the adult's only role in the political process is the pursuit of *internal* (private) benefits. The payment comes from the adult's *lifetime income*. The taxes can be regarded as supplying a revolving fund from which each individual draws during the period of life when his/her child is going to school. At other periods before marriage and in middle age or old age, the individual (as a nonparent) can be regarded as paying taxes in anticipation of "free" educational services, or for services previously received; but even when educating his/her children, the adult will be paying *some* current tax/price for them. The reason for such use of the tax system could be to obviate a capital market "imperfection" that prevents parents from drawing on their lifetime incomes. On this hypothesis the demand curves labeled D_k and ΣD disappear from Figure 1. The latter (dotted) demand curve can be replaced by the private (lifetime) demand curve D_j, which has shifted correspondingly to the right. Externalities need now *have no relevance for policy;* and we no longer need the joint supply reasoning. Meanwhile, compulsory laws can reduce any remaining uncertainty that any individual family will consume less than OQ_2.

The analysis of this model provides some useful insights for governments (like those of New York and Pennsylvania) that now seek a system of public finance of education that avoids the present "obstacle" of the religious clauses. If the assumptions of this second (capital market imperfection) model are made, the authorities could achieve the same results as the usual "free" system by replacing it with one that charged the parents full cost fees but also provided for a government-guaranteed loan scheme whereby the parents could borrow on their (the parents') future incomes to pay them. A government would then be supplying, not an educational service, but a financial one.[a] It is the government, not the court, who should explain the explicit functions and purposes of its intervention. Since previously there has been much vagueness on this point, there should be room for considerable rethinking and government initiative here. It is strongly arguable that financial convenience is broadly classifiable with those general welfare conveniences like bus transport, public health services, textbooks, and other nonideological services and facilities which were thought not to offend the Establishment clause in the *Everson*[11] and *Allen*[12] decisions. It is true that the Supreme Court, in the *Lemon*[13] and *Di Censo*[14] cases in 1971, emphasized the word "respecting" in the Establishment clause; and here the government financial service is not general, but relates to education which "visibly" affects religion. Nevertheless, the service is a general one to parents as a class; the benefit is not exclusively for "religious parents."

If religious parents in the present model were not prohibited from using the government loan scheme, they would not have to pay twice for their schooling (as they presently do) because all schools, public and private, would use positive prices covering full costs. Compare other public services that charge positive prices, and sometimes at full cost. Examples are

[a] If they did not face education taxes, young adults before marriage would be in a better position to save in anticipation of future education commitments. The loan system would thus be required for only part of the education expenses. In the nineteenth century, the whole of the financing was often handled in a "redistribution" within the extended family.

postal services, public transport systems, including road parking with meters and toll roads, and rented public housing. All these finance themselves by direct user charges (prices). The religious motorist who opts for private garaging of his car is not compelled to contribute to the payment of the nonreligious motorist who uses metered public parking. Similarly, in my second model, if education were financed with user charges, it would seem to be more difficult for the Supreme Court not to strike down schemes to make sectarian school patrons "pay twice" to subsidize the education of a nonreligious person in public schools. The effect would be economically the same as a discriminatory tax upon believers, and one that is used to subsidize nonbelievers. Clearly this would violate the Free Exercise clause.

Much of the argument remains when we replace the assumptions of the model with more realistic ones. Suppose we drop the assumption that families have identical incomes and that all adults have children. *Some* arguments based on externalities might now seem more plausible. For the moment I shall reinstate D_k, the neighbors' collective (community) demand curve in Figure 1. Assuming that the private demand for education is a positive function of income, we would have private demand curves for each family positioned farther to the left as its income decreased. The farther the demand curve D_j is to the left, the lower would be the private ability to share the cost. If moved far enough to the left, so that D_j intersects the horizontal axis at M for instance, this share becomes zero. In this case the community demand so dominates the private demand that to the individual families in question education becomes *genuinely* free. On the other hand, the farther to the right D_j moves, due to higher incomes, the larger the private share in the tuition cost would be. Beyond a certain income the parent would pay full cost. Where, for instance, D_j intersects the MC line at twice the distance of BG, the private demand would dominate the community demand. The *community* price would then be zero; the external benefits from this family's education would be intramarginal and received by the neighbors free of charge. Where incomes vary, the economically optimal arrangement is thus one with prices or tuitions that vary with family income. The only case where *all* family prices would be zero is where the community demand curve is so far to the right that it is in excess of the richest family's private demand curve at all points. Extraordinary weight will then be placed upon the aggregate external benefits, and the community demand will dominate *all* private demands.

If, however, the poor and the adults who never have children are both in minority sets, as they usually are, it would be most unlikely that the (childless) neighbors' aggregate demand curve could be so dominant (to the right). The rich and much of the middle-income groups could therefore still pay for their education out of lifetime incomes and pay full-cost positive

Table 1
Distribution of Taxes Supporting Public Education (as a Percent of Income), 1960 Census Year

All Taxes	Family Income				
	Under $2,000	$2,000- 2,999	$3,000 3,999	$4,000 4,999	$5,000- 5,999
Whites	7.83	4.72	4.00	3.69	3.59
Nonwhites	7.73	4.16	3.45	3.34	2.87

All Taxes	Family Income				
	$6,000- 6,999	$7,000- 7,999	$8,000- 9,999	$10,000- 14,999	Over $15,000
Whites	3.37	3.00	2.53	2.14	2.63
Nonwhites	2.61	2.55	2.48	2.83	3.08

Source: W. Norton Grubb, "The Distribution of Costs and Benefits in an Urban Public School System," *National Tax Journal*, Vol. XXIV, No. 1, March 1971, Table 1.

prices—especially if a loan system were established. Even the poor, especially with the aid of a loan scheme, could pay a significant fraction of their education cost as a direct price. Notice that such a scheme need not alter any redistributive provisions featured in the existing system. We need to discover what education taxes are presently being paid by the poor. These can then be abolished, and in their place user charges can be substituted.

Real world evidence shows that the very poorest do indeed pay for education through significant property taxes. Table 1 gives percentages of income paid and shows that tax incidence was clearly regressive in Massachusetts at the time of one recent study of Boston. The poorest group was paying nearly 8 percent of its current income on education taxes. If the part of these education taxes (rich and poor) deemed to cover private benefits were collected directly, as user tax prices, at the door of the school, then even if some of these prices did not cover full cost, there would be, for reasons already explained, considerable relief to parochial schools compared with the present financing system, and probably a much larger relief then the modest parochial "aid" attemped recently (see the section entitled "The Nyquist Case").

To complete this theoretical section, it is necessary to refer to one remaining argument in favor of providing "free" education—even to the rich. This is the argument for social mixing: Under a free system everybody, hopefully, will go to the same sort of schools. Two further arguments are connected: (l) "social cohesion" will be achieved; (2) there are educational benefits to poor children from being taught in the presence of rich children. Belief in the social cohesion argument usually rests on a personal value judgment. The typical advocates usually deny that they want to impose their own tastes. They usually insist that "social mixing" is what *society* wants. The test of this notion is surely some form of majority expression in the legislature. In the political body of New York State, the case that this article centers upon, there *is* a clearly articulated expression of preference on this matter. But it is a request for a move toward pluralism, diversity, and family choice [a development that is welcomed by the Supreme Court: see *Nyquist,* page 2966 (4)]. This being the case, there seems to be no remaining argument that could oppose significant switching from taxes to positive pricing in education.

The Nyquist Case

Evidence that several states have the political desire to aid parochial and other nonpublic schools is now considerable. One significant motive is the self-interest of the public schools themselves. If nonpublic schools fail financially and become extinct, and if budgets for public schools cannot be greatly expanded (especially in near bankrupt New York City), then parochial school students will pour into the public schools, increase the pressure on their space and personnel, and thereby lower quality. The main reason for the threat to the survival of nonpublic schools is rising costs, especially personnel costs. Education is labor-intensive. Teachers, and even administrators, are becoming more strongly organized. School expenditures per student in America have increased fivefold *in real* (price-deflated) *terms* in three decades.[15] Nonpublic schools have not been able to keep pace with such increases, even with increased tuition, and quality has fallen. Moreover, the cost difference to families between using private and using public schools continues to worsen, and the numbers of children involved are huge in some areas. New York State, for example, has some 700,000 nonpublic school students—20 percent of total enrollment—facing the possibility of transferring to the public system.

It may be argued that these circumstances provide opportunities for significant strategic behavior on the part of the religious groups. They could threaten to reduce their private educational output, thus threatening increases in the cost of public education. Moreover, if we drop the "fixed proportions" version of the joint supply model wherein there is a fixed amount of literacy produced for a fixed amount of religion, in favor of a variable proportions version we can envisage some strategic behavior in the following sense. The amount of religious inculcation per unit of secular education might be seen by religious school interests as a variable that can be determined in political bargaining. On its own terms, such an argument seems weak because the biggest strategic guns are with the politicians representing 80 percent of the voters, people who don't use parochial schools. But, on whatever side the strategy lies, there is some exchange or trade that remains to be made. The central question here is the constitutional legality of the trade, however imperfect. Moreover, even if the quantity of religious inculcation *is* no longer fixed, the appropriate model is still joint supply, even though it is the variable proportions case—like wool and mutton in the economics textbook. In this version it is possible to vary the degree of the one output relative to the jointly produced one. However, it is still not possible to produce one output to the two goods (wool or Bible reading) without *some* of the other (mutton or literacy). The Supreme Court seems to think that complete separation *is* possible. Because I believe the case to be one of joint production, even with variable proportions, the purchaser of the one commodity is *not* subsidizing (aiding) the purchaser of the other.

Now let us return to the evidence. Whatever the degree of political strategy involved, New York State (in 1972) passed into law three programs that offered some financial relief to nonpublic elementary and secondary schools. The first provided for direct money grants to qualifying nonpublic schools for maintenance and repair of facilities and equipment to ensure the "health, welfare and safety of students." To qualify, a nonpublic school had to be nonprofit and serve a high concentration of pupils from low-income families. The annual grant was a modest $30 per pupil, or $40 if the facilities were more than 25 years old, and could not exceed 50 percent of the average per-pupil cost for equivalent services in the public schools. Legislative findings concluded that (1) the state "has a primary responsibility to ensure the health, welfare and safety of children attending . . . non-public schools"; (2) the "fiscal crisis in non-public education . . . has caused a diminution of proper maintenance and repair programs, threatening the health, welfare and safety of nonpublic school children" in low-income urban areas; and (3) "a healthy and safe school environment" contributes "to the stability of urban neighborhoods." Section 2 established a tuition reimbursement plan for parents of children attending non-public elementary or secondary schools. To qualify, the parent's annual taxable income had to be less than $5,000. The amount of reimbursement was $50 per grade school child and $100 per high school student as long as those amounts did not exceed 50 percent of actual tuition paid. The legislature asserted that (1) the right to select among alternative educational systems should be available in a pluralistic society, and (2) a sharp decline in nonpublic school pupils would massively increase public school enrollment and costs and seriously jeopardize quality education for all children.

Reiterating a declaration contained in the first section, the legislature concluded that "such assistance is clearly secular, neutral and nonideological."

The third program was designed to give tax relief to parents failing to qualify for tuition reimbursement. Each eligible taxpayer-parent was entitled to deduct a stipulated sum from the adjusted gross income for each child attending nonpublic school. The amount of the deduction was unrelated to the amount of tuition actually paid and decreased as the amount of taxable income increased. These sections were also prefaced by a series of legislative assertions similar to those accompanying the previous sections. Of the 700,000 students in New York attending nonpublic schools, approximatley 85 percent attend church-affiliated schools. About 80 percent of the schools entitled to receive maintenance and repair grants were Catholic and taught Catholic doctrine to some degree.

On June 25, 1973, the District Court held in the *Nyquist* case that the maintenance and repair grants and the tuition-reimbursement grants were invalid, but that the income tax provisions did not violate the Constitution's Establishment clause. The Supreme Court later rejected all three aid provisions, on grounds of a well-defined three-part test that evolved from the Court's previous considerations of the Establishment clause cases. To be valid, nonpublic school aid must henceforth (1) reflect a clearly secular legislative purpose, (2) have a primary effect that neither advances nor inhibits religion, and (3) avoid "excessive" government entanglement with religion. The New York legislation in question was considered acceptable on the first test. The "maintenance and repair" assistance failed on the second test, however, because it had "a primary effect that advances religion in that it subsidizes directly the religious activities of sectarian elementary and secondary schools."[16] The state officials had argued that their "maintenance and repair" provisions were similar to other expenditures approved by the Court, especially bus fares to public and nonpublic schools (*Everson*), and secular textbooks (*Allen*). The Court's reply was that in these cases the aid was successfully channeled to secular activities without providing direct aid to sectarian aspects of schooling. Furthermore,

It is true that such aid served indirectly and incidentally to promote the religious function by rendering it more likely that children would attend sectarian schools and by freeing the budgets of those schools for use in other non-secular areas. But an indirect and incidental effect beneficial to religious instituions has never been thought a sufficient defect to warrant the invalidation of a state law."[17]

The Court argued that the New York "maintenance and repair" provision lacked the specifically articulated secular restrictions that were contained in *Everson* and *Allen*. It therefore could not be assured that the primary effect was not to subsidize religion.

To an economist, the apparent confusion in the Court's reasoning stems from its failure to identify the "product" that New York State was in fact trying to purchase. As outlined above, there are several possible products: private benefits of education, external benefits of education, and the "financial convenience" which enables a family to purchase education for its children through taxes (on its lifetime income). It is up to governments to state clearly the purposes of their legislation. Suppose the *main* argument for intervention is the purchase of external benefits. Ignoring the financial benefits for the moment, the joint supply model is appropriate. The two jointly supplied outputs are religious inculcation and literacy benefits (for example, crime reduction). The government should be buying strictly the latter and should not be concerned with production itself. If for some reason the government wanted to purchase beef while "keeping its distance" from hide purchasers, it would concern itself with the end product only. As the arguments in the first section of this paper have indicated, it should not arrange complicated subsidies for the cattle-raising industry and send in inspectors to make sure that government money went exclusively into the production of the beef part of the animal and not the hides. Moreover, the action of becoming a purchaser of beef does not have the "primary effect" of favoring the hide consumers any more than the action of purchasing hides has the "primary" effect of favoring beef consumers. With joint production there are no *primary* effects, only *joint* effects. And as mentioned earlier, the purchase of one product does not mean the *subsidization* of the other.

If the purchase of external benefits is in fact the main rationale of state intervention in eduation, it is unfortunate that the earlier decisions of *Everson* and *Allen* threw out misleading signals to those like New York State who wanted, constitutionally, to purchase education outputs from nonpublic schools. Indeed, there is no economic difference in terms of resource outcomes between (1) the government's purchasing external benefits by confining its payments to maintenance and repair (or bus rides and textbooks, etc.) and (2) simply paying the school fees directly. The results are the same: both increased religious education *and* more non-religious education are produced. As children read the Bible, they become more literate. As they become more literate, greater external benefits (for example, crime reduction) are created.

The Nyquist court also struck down New York's system of tuition subsidies and income tax benefits, not on the grounds that the attempts to confine them to secular aspects were unconvincing or impracticable, but that no such attempt was actually made. This demonstrates most clearly to the economist the Court's failure to appreciate the inherent joint supply relationship between secular and sectarian education. As long as the Court's reasoning in *Nyquist* continues to dominate, the obstacles to improving the financial position of the parochial schools via the conventional methods seem insurmountable. State governments are reproached, as in the *Nyquist* case, if they do not financially separate the secular education from the sectarian. Yet when they do, they are opposed on grounds of becoming "excessively" entangled with religion, in a way that involves a "comprehensive, discriminating, and continuing state of surveillance."[18]

It will be helpful to consider next the *Nyquist* decision in the light of the other government objective in intervention: providing individuals with financial facilities to rearrange their lifetime spending in favor of their own children's education. This is the "financial convenience" argument metioned above. One inhibition to the Court's acceptance of this objective fleetingly suggests itself. From the tone of the language, one sometimes gets a judicial view of the state as an entity independent of the individuals in society which enjoys a tax-financed income (called "public money") that is equally detached. Traces of this view no doubt have an historical basis. At the time of independence in 1776, the predominant relation between religion and the state in England—a relation which the American founding fathers wished to avoid in their new constitution—was that of one selected, established church that was sponsored and supported by the Crown, an official monopoly church. The debate was thus cast in terms of the discretionary power of a nondemocratic monarchic regime to favor or disfavor particular religions. It is an easy step for constitutional lawyers to continue the same currency of language. The court's arguments in *Nyquist* on the subject of tax credits or tax deductions[19] give the best indication of this historical carry-over. To understand the carry-over fully, consider the extreme case where government presumes that it owns the whole national income. If the government chooses to tax none of it, then the whole of an individual's income can be regarded as a huge tax exemption, deduction, or subsidy. Where the Supreme Court views tax exemptions as subsidies (i.e., aid), it would be impossible for *any* organized religion to survive under the U.S. Constitution. The Separation clause would then, in effect, be a "wall of exclusion," not a wall of mere "separation."

The reasoning in *Nyquist* clearly treats tax exemptions as "aid." The Court struck down New York's planned system of tax exemptions because of the following reasons:

In practical terms there would appear to be little difference, for purposes of determining whether such aid has the affect of advancing religion, between the tax benefit allowed here and the tuition grant. . . . The only difference is that one parent receives an actual cash payment while the other is allowed to reduce by an arbitrary amount *the sum he would otherwise be obliged to pay over to the State*.[20]

While there is no suggestion that the Court believes government owns the whole of national income, there is a tacit belief that it knows precisely what proportion of it *is* so owned, or commandeered, in the last quoted sentence where it refers to the sum that the individual would "otherwise be obliged to pay over to the State." It is difficult to see the authority for this statement. In a democracy the pattern of tax obligations to the state is decided by votes; there is no mechanical way of predicting the outcome of that decision, and tax obligations can be allowed by democratic governments to vary over time and between groups in a way that no court can have advanced knowledge of.

The Supreme Court acknowledged that the New York appellees relied upon the *Walz v. Tax Commission*[21] decision in 1970 in which New York's property tax exemption for religious organizations was upheld. It decided that *Walz* in fact provided no support. The Court nevertheless neglected to refer to the most relevant part of the reasoning in *Walz:*

The grant of a tax exemption is not sponsorship since the government does not transfer part of its revenue to churches but simply abstains from demanding that the church support the state. No one has ever suggested that tax exemption has converted libraries, art galleries, or hospitals into the arms of the state or put employees "on the public payroll." There is no genuine nexus between tax exemption and establishment of religion.[22]

The *Nyquist* judges thus appeared to view the state as something separate from its individual members. Similarly, they seemed to treat "religion" as an abstraction or disembodied entity. "Religious activity" can be viewed, on the contrary, as having no meaning unless it pertains to the behavior of identifiable individuals. The church is a collection or interaction of individuals with common beliefs. Seen in this light, there is no difference between exempting the church from taxes and exempting its individual members. In the *Nyquist* case, the Court nevertheless distinguished the decision in *Walz* as one which provided a *general* offset to state hostility (via taxation) to "the Church." The New York tax benefits, in contrast, were viewed as *special* benefits because they went to individuals who sent their children to sectarian schools and thus "advanced" religious institutions. The "aid" in *Walz,* the *Nyquist* court argued, was different because it was "a product not of any purpose to support or to subsidize, but of a fiscal relationship designed to minimize involvement and entanglement between Church and State.[23]

Its acknowledgment of the *Walz* judgment that the church's property should be exempt, for whatever reason, obviously precluded the *Nyquist* court from the extreme view that government owns all the national income. Yet the boundaries between government and individual income were left ambiguous. If "religion" is defined as pertaining only to identifiable individuals, the question involves the extent to which the income of these individuals should be encroached upon or left alone. Consider the question according to the "benefit principle" in public finance, in which taxes are viewed as payments from individuals or groups for particular benefits rendered those same individuals or groups. Religious individuals enjoy wealth and income in two forms: first, in the form of common property held, for instance, in the shape of church buildings; second, in the form of direct personal income from work. The *Walz* decision was made with respect to the first category in church property. On the "benefit principle" there is a much stronger case for taxing church property than for taxing the income of sectarian parents. Church property receives important benefits from certain expensive government activities such as police and fire protection. If the government refused these services to the church, the church would be obliged to purchase them privately. Allowing churches to be "free riders" on various public services amounts to aid in kind, and this aid *does* help to directly subsidize religion.

Next, according to the "benefit principle" of public finance, taxes on an individual's lifetime income should be in proportion to the benefits of "free" education that he or she enjoys. Insofar as sectarian parents do not use "free" public schools but are nonetheless compelled to contribute taxes to pay for them, these taxes can be regarded as constituting a "hostility" to religion and violating the Free Exercise clause of the Constitution. The correct remedy is not to offset this hostility with tax exemptions on church *property,* but to remove the hostility directly by granting tax exemptions to sectarian *parents.* The anomaly is that church property receives benefits and pay no taxes, while sectarian parents receive no private benefits from public education yet pay taxes for it. To cover the externalities, tax liabilities on parents of sectarian school children should be in proportion only to the external benefits.

Resolution of the Problem

This section is concerned with positive economics which attempts to predict ways that economic problems might get resolved in view of real world constraints. The "problem" here is mainly a conflict between the political needs of a state government and the Supreme Court's "roadblock" of constitutional interpretation. It is desirable first to pose the problem in the toughest terms and then to attempt to suggest possible ways that might be predicted to solve it. I shall assume that the *Nyquist* interpretation of the law continues in force, and that state laws continue to face the severe constraint of having to (1) reflect a secular purpose, (2) neither advance nor inhibit religion as a "primary" effect, and (3) avoid "excessive" government entanglement with religion.

The first avenue to explore is the possibility of the state's granting direct financial aid (for example, school vouchers) not to one class of families, such as those with children in nonpublic schools, but to all families, with this aid spendable in public or nonpublic schools. It might be argued that such a system would have the primary effect of giving free choice to all, not just to sectarian parents. If most parents used their new freedom of choice to select from the public system, the proportion of all parents choosing sectarian schools would still be in the minority, so that the "primary" effect would not be to favor them.[24] This argument might be most persuasive if a voucher system were phased in, so that vouchers could be used only within the public system at first. (The voucher system that has been adopted for three districts in New Hampshire for the fall of 1975 has excluded parochial schools following legal advice.) Secular private schools could be added next, and sectarian schools last of all. *Nyquist*, in contrast, had to deal not with a global change in the system, but with a marginal change—and one that focused upon the net effect on parochial schools only.

It would appear that such a (voucher) policy would face considerable uncertainty. The new phased-in system would still be vulnerable. When parochial schools are eventually included, this last phase might be individually struck down on the grounds that it had a "primary" effect in favor of religion. The use of the word "primary" in *Nyquist* is not entirely clear to me, although this may possibly be due to my lack of legal expertise. In the opening three-part test, a "primary" effect was certainly stressed; but in the subsequent reasoning, which referred only to the "effect" test, the Court observed:

What we have said demonstrates that New York's maintenance and repair provisions violate the Establishment Clause because their effect, inevitably, is to subsidize and advance the religious mission of sectarian schools.[25]

Furthermore, the *Nyquist* court was at pains to quote Justice Black in *Everson*:

No tax in any amount, large or small, can be levied to support any religious activities or institutions, whatever form they may adopt to teach or practice religion.[26]

What to me contains the most cryptic comment on the "primary" effect notion is footnote 39 of *Nyquist*. Responding therein to the new view of the appellees that the central question was whether the primary effect of the New York program would subsidize religion or promote legitimate secular objectives, the Court replied:

We do not think that such metaphysical judgements are either possible or necessary. Our cases simply do not support the notion that a law found to have "primary" effect to promote some legitimate end under the State's police power is immune from further examination to ascertain whether it also has the direct and immediate effect of advancing religion.

Clearly the Court has also used the words "direct," "immediate," and "inevitable" as important adjectives describing "effect." It seems relevant to me that the Court was not impressed by the argument that the New York aid was directed not to the schools, but to the children via their parents. The Court was concerned that *any* of the money might "get to," or benefit, parochial schools. The cumulative effect of this reasoning seems in my (admittedly fallible) judgment to constitute potential judicial hostility to any voucher plan that includes parochial schools.

Suppose, however, that I am wrong in the above assessment. Assume that the universal voucher scheme passed the "primary" or "direct" effect test. The Court could still prohibit it on the reasoning of "excessive entanglement." Most voucher schemes that have been discussed call for considerable administrative supervision, such as their policing and fulfilling school access conditions. Accusations of excessive entanglement could easily follow. Moreover, *Nyquist* emphasized more than administrative entanglement. It pointed to the "grave potential" for entanglement of continuing political strife over aid to religion. The Court quoted Justice Harlan that "What is at stake . . . is preventing that kind and degree of government involvement in religious life that, as history teaches us, is apt to lead to strife and frequently strain a political system to the breaking point."[27] It observed that although the New York aid scheme started out at modest levels "we know from long experience . . . that aid programs of any kind become entrenched, to escalate in cost, and to generate their own aggressive constituencies. And the larger the class of recipients, the greater the pressure for accelerated increases."[28] There is already, of course, a strong education lobby for the present system. The fear with a system of universal vouchers spendable in *any* school is that the lobby will now be joined by religious forces.[b] A religious lobby may become so conspicuous in politics that opposition to it, and perhaps opposition to the continuation of the vouchers it enjoys, might threaten to develop, in the eyes of the Court, into "political strife."

I believe there is another avenue that is much more promising. I explain this initially by focusing upon the preferences of the key or median (middle) voters. I assume that the political will to aid parochial schools in New York reflects especially the preferences of such voters and that they are located within the 80 percent of families who use the public schools. The New York government gave two motives for its parochial aid plan: (1) the need for a plural society and diversity, and (2) the need to prevent the overburdening of public schools with the parochial schools' population. I shall assume that

---

[b] Several New Hampshire sectarian institutions have already sued the state for the right to participate in the voucher program beginning in 1975.

the second motive is the stronger. It is consistent with the self-interest of the "key" voters and public school users to want to avoid an increase in school taxes and the drop in educational quality of a classroom that is overcrowded with large numbers of student "refugees" from bankrupt parochial schools. To avoid this, the same public school users are willing to pay up to some maximum "price." This maximum price is not necessarily as high as the average cost of a public school student's education, which means that it is not as high in value as Milton Friedman's type of voucher system would provide.[29] Evidence that the relevant price the key voters are willing to pay is much lower than average cost of education is suggested from the New York program's offerings to parochial schools of fairly modest benefit.

I shall argue that the appropriate way for the public school user to pay the optimal "price" is not to tax public and nonpublic users and then refund the latter, but to try to institute marginal user taxes on the former. They could be introduced gradually as follows. All schools expect cost increases in future. A state government could decree that the required *increases* in tax revenue could fall exclusively on that section of society that uses public schools. This scheme could not be described by the Supreme Court as a planned subsidy to parochial schools from a static sum of "public money." "Public money" has to be increased, and that calls for a separate decision. Increases in the common pool of "public money" are determined according to the particular mix of taxes that is selected. Such taxation patterning meanwhile is the prerogative of the state government. In the past, a wide variety of tax maneuvers met previous cost increases. The number of taxes that has accumulated in the effort to meet rising education costs in Massachusetts, for instance, is now eleven.[30] A user tax would make it twelve.

I offer the above proposal as the best practical innovation, and I "predict" it will succeed and stand on its own. My second, more "radical" approach to be described next is not to be taken as the inevitable successor or likelier prospect than the first. It is offered more in a speculative vein. There is no obligation in the federal Constitution that a state government must provide education. A state government could therefore announce that it was to terminate its education system altogether, say in July of next year. This step alone could "get money to the parochial schools" in a perfectly legal way; taxes would be reduced, and parochial school families would cease paying twice. Soon after, say in two months, the government could introduce a "globally" new educational system, open to all, but significantly financed by user taxes, like many other publicly provided services. The Supreme Court could not argue that parochial parents were being enabled to pay increased parochial fees from their incomes with "money that would otherwise have gone to public education" because this implies that the Court and not the government can prescribe the correct amount of money that "should" go to public education. Indeed, it would be just as logical for a court to condemn a public system on the Free Exercise constitutional grounds that it was financed with money that "would otherwise have gone" to parochial schools.

With this method of rebuilding the whole system anew, there would be more flexibility to adjust the user taxes in accordance with the median voter's optimal "price" of avoiding an influx of sectarian families into his public schools. It should be observed that this could eventually do more than absolve sectarian families from paying *extra* taxes to finance parochial school cost increases; it could also considerably reduce the tax burden from its previous level. Meanwhile, if each school were financed partly, but significantly, with user tax funds from the student customers it could attract, the new system would go a long way to stimulating the sort of competition that voucher proponents desire. Every time a family withdrew its child from a public school it would automatically withdraw funds (supplied by user taxes) and place pressure on the school to improve according to parental preferences in self-defense. Even if the change were confined to the principle that all future cost *increases* are to be born by user taxes, judging by the rate of recent cost increases, the user tax would soon be a considerable fraction of the total costs. As time went on, it would be appropriate for government to introduce a family loan system. This system could partly replace the present method of collecting from lifetime incomes through lifetime taxes. Superficially this would look to some like a voucher system. But if so, there would be much more clarity about what the "vouchers" were. They would be advances on an individual's own future income, not "aid" from some remote third party.

I conclude by anticipating the objection that a policy of charging families directly for private educational benefits might run into special constitutional limitations. In a note in *Rodriguez* the Court intimated that a tuition charge at public school might unconstitutionally discriminate against the poor if it had the effect of excluding them from minimum of public education.[31] In *Johnson v. New York State Education Department* it was alleged that a school textbook fee was unconstitutional if nonpayment resulted in denial of the books because this could prevent a child from having a proper education. The Court, however, avoided deciding the case on the grounds of mootness.[32]

I shall make seven observations on this issue. First I have been referring in this essay to user *taxes*, not to fees. An argument that low-income groups cannot afford any kind of taxes, user or otherwise, has to meet the fact that the very poorest are *already paying* substantial educational taxes. (See Tables 1 and 2.) A switch to user taxes only makes this more explicit. With more competition keeping costs lower, many poor persons would probably end up paying less than now. It is incorrect to believe that if people are

Table 2
Absolute Dollar Contributions of Whites to Public Education (in 1960)

				Family Income					
	$2,000	$2,000-2,999	$3,000-3,999	$4,000-4,999	$5,000-5,999	$6,000-6,999	$7,000-7,999	$8,000-9,999	$10,000-14,999
Contribution	$117	118	140	166	197	219	225	215	268

Source: Calculations made of percentages in Table 1 applied to median income of each column.

prevented from paying *direct* charges to finance increased costs, then they escape burden because they will be burdened *indirectly* through (1) higher tax payments and/or (2) lower-quality schooling of their children when parochial students crowd their classrooms. Second, the fact that educational user taxes would be compulsory prevents parents from refusing their children an education. Third, education itself is compulsory, and this is a second line of defense against nonpayment. Fourth, even if the allegation were true that public school user taxes *were* antipoor, it is entirely possible that the present system whereby parochial school parents pay *twice* is even more antipoor. The average income of parochial school users is below average in New York State. A policy of *opposition* to public school user taxes designed to reduce the average sectarian family's burden of paying twice would itself be antipoor in this sense. Fifth, even if further income redistribution in favor of the poor were required, there are a host of other presumably superior ways of doing it. These include a negative income tax system, increases in welfare payments, and decreases in regressive taxes and excises. Concern for the poor does not prevent the continuation of a flat price system in other public services such as the post office, public transit, toll road usage, and metered public parking. Sixth, even if the above arguments were still not cogent enough, a case for not charging the poor for education does not apply to the vast (and growing) majority of families who are not poor.

Seventh, and last, recent court cases have attached some importance to historical tradition.[33] The case for user taxes in New York State, however, would not seem to be damaged on these grounds. Education in public schools in New York has certainly been free of user charges to the public for about a century. For nearly a century before that, however, educational user taxes, then called "rate bills," were paid by all income groups. There is, incidentally, no simple causative connection between the earlier user charges and the lower levels of nineteenth-century education compared with twentieth-century. All countries had lower levels of education in the last century, however it was financed. The major explanation for lower educational quantity in the nineteenth century was lower incomes.[34] And before it can be claimed that the rate bills were antipoor, they have to be compared with the alternative sources of finance that were used after their abolition in 1876, sources that included severely regressive indirect taxes.

Notes

1. Kenneth Mott and Stephen Edelstein, "Church, State and Education," *Journal of Law and Education*, 2(4): October 1973, pp. 535-591.

2. Leo Pfeffer, "Freedom and Separation: America's Constitution to Civilization," *Journal of Church and State* 108, 1960.

3. R. Drinan, "The Novel 'Liberty' Created by the McCollum Decision" 39 Georgia Law Journal.

4. Phillip Kurland, *Religion and the Law*, The Law School, U of Chicago, Chicago, 1962.

5. W. Katz, "Religion and The Law," in *Religious Perspectives in American Culture*, North Western University Press, Chicago, 1961.

6. *The Committee for Public Education and Religious Liberty v. Nyquist*, 413 U.S. 756, 93 S.Ct. 2055 (1973), hereafter cited *Nyquist*.

7. Recent analysis by economists concludes that compulsory laws have largely endorsed what parents would do anyway, or, in other words, that negligence in the sense of failure to secure an education for their children is at most nontypical.
W.M. Landes and L.C. Solmon, "Compulsory Schooling Legislation: An Economic Analysis of the Law and Social Change in the Nineteenth Century," *Journal of Economic History*, March 1972.
E.G. West, "The Political Economy of American Public School Legislation," *Journal of Law and Economics* 101: 124 (1967).

8. The classic exposition is in Mark V. Pauly, "Mixed Public and Private Financing of Education," *American Economic Review*, 57(1): March 1967.

9. Harold Demsetz, "Joint Supply and Price Discrimination," *Journal of Law and Economics*, April 1974, p. 390.

10. *Walz v. Tax Commission*, 397 U.S. (1970) at 674.

11. *Everson v. Board of Education*, 330 U.S. 1 (1947).

12. *Board of Education v. Allen*, 392 U.S. 236 (1968).

13. *Lemon v. Kurtzman*, 403 U.S. 602 (1971).

14. *Early v. Di Censo*, 403 U.S. 602 (1971).

15. James W. Guthrie, "Public Control of Public Schools: Can We Get

It Back?'' *Public Affairs Report*, Institute of Governmental Studies, University of California, Berkeley. June 1974, No. 3.

16. *Nyquist*, at 2966.

17. *Nyquist*, at 2967.

18. *Lemon v. Kurtzman*, 403 U.S. at 619.

19. *Nyquist*, Section C at 2973.

20. *Nyquist*, at 2974, our italics.

21. 397 U.S. at 664. Decided May 4, 1970.

22. 397 U.S. at 675.

23. *Nyquist*, at 2976.

24. Stephen D. Sugarman, "Family Choice: The Next Step in the Quest for Equal Educational Opportunity?" The Law School, University of California at Berkeley, unpublished private manuscript, Chapter 5. My reference however does not do full justice to Sugarman's argument—which relies more on the *Walz* case than on *Nyquist*.

25. *Nyquist*, at 2969.

26. 330 U.S. at 16.

27. *Nyquist*, at 2977.

28. *Nyquist*, at 2979.

29. Milton Friedman, *Capitalism and Freedom*, U. of Chicago, Chicago, 1962. "The Voucher Idea," *New York Times Magazine*, September 23, 1973.

30. Norton Grubb, "The Distribution of Costs and Benefits in an Urban Public School System," *National Tax Journal*, vol. XXIV, no. 1, March 1971, Table 1, p. 3.

31. 411 U.S. at 25 note 60. The Research Paper: Student Fees, Centre for Law and Education (Harvard University) Cambridge, Mass. (1972) develops a battery of arguments in the *Rodriguez* direction.

32. 409 U.S. 75 (1972).

33. See especially *Walz*, 397 U.S. at 675, 676.

34. E.G. West, "Education Slowdown and Public Intervention in 19th Century England: A Study in the Economics of Bureaucracy," *Explorations in Economic History*, January, 1975, Vol. 12, No. 1, pp. 61-87.

Can Government Aid Private Schools?

Roger A. Freeman

Despairing of the legal viability of other methods of governmental aid to church-affiliated schools, in "Economic Analysis of the Law and Politics of Nonpublic School Aid" E.G. West advances a novel idea on how to achieve the desired goal. He refers to repeated attempts by several states to assist such schools financially and discusses some of the decisions of the U.S. Supreme Court between 1971 and 1974 which declared such aid to be unconstitutional, even if it is restricted to certain secular activities, to grants to families paying tuition to such schools, or to tax benefits to such families. The discouraging record of those decisions did not end the quest of protagonists of private schools for obtaining some form of direct or indirect assistance from government. But it left them without a specific program to pursue because virtually all the various methods that had been proposed in recent years were held by the Court to be violative of the "no establishment" clause of the First Amendment to the Constitution, some directly, some by implication or clear indication in some of the decisions. Thus the Court seems to have blocked virtually all avenues to effective governmental assistance for church-affiliated schools—or for parents who support those schools—save a constitutional amendment. But the chances of passing such an amendment through both houses of Congress with a two-thirds majority and through the requisite number of state legislatures (38) are, at this time, realistically speaking, nil. This leaves the private school forces "all dressed up but with no place to go."

The problem itself exists and is getting worse, with private schools closing at a rapid rate and a growing number of parents being forced to send their children to a public school. If current trends continue, the public schools within a short time will enjoy a monopoly on grade and high school education—as they already have in many areas—except for a small and declining number of families who are in a fortunate location or financially blessed. An influx of several million children will, of course, add heavily to the taxpayer's burden of supporting the public schools.

Now E.G. West advances a novel idea on how to bridge the gap. If public funds cannot be channeled to church-affiliated schools, whether directly or through the parents, and if the taxes of families paying tuition to private schools cannot be lowered, then maybe the taxes of families with children in public schools can be raised. That would give families with children in nonpublic schools a relative financial advantage. They would save some money compared with families of children in public school. This

28

would, at least in part, offset the fees they pay to the nonpublic school their children attend.

West proposes (pages 23 and 24) either that states impose required *increases* in school tax revenues on "that section of society that uses public schools" or that a state government "stop its education system altogether" and soon after introduce a new educational system, open to all, but significantly financed by user taxes. It is an appealing thought—at least to those who favor nonpublic schools—which does not run afoul of the Supreme Court's restrictions on aid to private schools.

West's plan would sail between the Scylla of "supporting religious activities" and the Charybdis of "excessive entanglement" between church and state. It would (1) channel no public funds to private schools, nor to parents; (2) not reduce the taxes of families with children in nonpublic schools; and (3) not entangle government with religious schools. Yet it would give some financial encouragement to attendance at private schools by making it more expensive to send children to a public school.

The question is: *Will it work?*

West considers the possibility of a federal constitutional challenge (p. 35) because the Court in *Rodriguez* raised the question of whether tuition charges at public schools might unconstitutionally discriminate against the poor.[a] He disposes of it quickly: "The particular questions raised by such utterances can easily be met. First we have been referring in this article to user *taxes*, not to fees. An argument that low income groups cannot afford any kind of taxes, user or otherwise, simply cannot withstand scrutiny. The very poorest are already paying substantial education taxes."

A reading of the Court's statement (see footnote below) suggests that it is more than a casual obiter dictum, that it is intended as a warning to legislators. If the question arose, the Court would not treat it lightly and, in all likelihood, take a serious view of the imposition of a mandatory fee— whether called and levied as a tax or not—upon attendance at a public school. West is correct in saying that the poor are paying substantial education taxes—if they own property subject to taxation or purchase goods subject to sales taxation used for educational purposes, etc. But they pay those taxes as the owners of property or as purchasers of goods on a uniform basis with others. That is different from having to pay a tax for sending one's children to a public school.

---

[a] *San Antonio v. Rodriguez*, 411 U.S. 1 (1973) at 25, footnote 60: "An educational finance system might be hypothesized, however, in which the analogy to the wealth discrimination cases would be considerably closer. If elementary and secondary education were made available by the State only to those able to pay a tuition assessed against each pupil, there would be a clearly defined class of 'poor' people—defined in terms of their inability to pay the prescribed sum—who would be absolutely precluded from receiving an education. That case would present a far more compelling set of circumstances for judicial assistance than the case before us today."

West mentions in passing (page 25) that free public schools have been established for about a century, but he does not seem to realize how much of an article of faith free public schools have become to the American public. Twenty-five state constitutions specifically ordain the maintenance of "free" public schools while another twenty-three state constitutions refer to public school systems in similar, and largely synonymous, terms. (Only Georgia and South Carolina have eliminated the requirement of public education from their constitutions.)

West never mentions the state constitutional requirement of public schools—and *free* public schools. I have little doubt but that the supreme courts of most states would find a law imposing user taxes on attendance at public schools to be unconstitutional. I doubt, however, that such a judicial test will come about: no state legislature could be persuaded to impose such a tax. In fact, West may have difficulty finding a sponsor for such a bill among state legislators. What I believe he underrates is the depth and strength of the tradition of *free* public schools.

The "rate bills" which West mentions (page 25), by which school patrons paid school costs over a century ago, are referred to in current literature as examples of a bygone and benighted age. A serious public proposal to reintroduce them—which is what West in effect suggests— would cause an uproar that would drown out such plans. Even in public higher education the principle of paying for attendance is under severe attack, tuition accounts for a steadily declining share of the cost of instruction, and demands are rising for a gradual diminution and abolition of tuitions, at least in *public* higher education. One example is the student aid bill H.R. 3471 just introduced by the chairman of the House Subcommittee on Postsecondary Education, Representative James O'Hara, which would make large state incentive grants available at "zero tuition" institutions.

I want to make it clear that personally I favor tuitions which are more nearly commensurate with the cost of instruction. But realistically, that just is not in the cards in today's atmosphere. West's plan is a fascinating intellectual exercise, and I could say much in its favor. Unfortunately, it has, in my opinion, no chance of being carried out.

This does not mean that we must necessarily give up on getting aid for private schools, though it certainly has become a much harder task since the *Nyquist* decision. But I am not so sure—as West seems to be—that the *Nyquist* decision is the last word in the private school aid controversy, although it happens to be the latest word at this time.

The West article is divided into three sections preceded by an introduction: (1) a theoretical analysis ("Educational Public Goods and Optimal Subsidies"), (2) a discussion of the Nyquist case, and (3) a development of his own proposal ("Resolution of the Problem").

In the introduction West calls the religion clause in the First Amendment "ambiguous." To strict constructionists it is not at all ambiguous. It means to them exactly what it says and no more: that Congress shall pass no law to establish a religion—which is very understandable at a time when some of the states (not to mention the motherland) did have a state religion—and that Congress could not prohibit free exercise of religion—at a time when the memory of restriction of free exercise of religion in some of the colonies (and the motherland) was still quite alive.

But in a series of decisions, most of them divided 5:4 or 6:3, the Supreme Court has interpreted the "no establishment" clause as meaning more, and it has zigzagged in saying just how much more, with fluctuating majorities—and sometimes the minority in one case writes the majority opinion of the next case.

It will probably be best to leave a discussion of those decisions to a review of the second section, which deals with the Nyquist case.

I cannot say that I find the first section, which is intended to establish a theoretical basis, very impressive nor the models and metaphors particularly persuasive. A much better case for giving public support to nonpublic schools has been made by several authors and in various official documents. The author refers several times to a reduction of crime as a result of education or literacy (pages 4, 6, 7 . . .). What proof is there of a positive or causative relationship? Literacy has certainly increased in the United States (i.e., illiteracy has steadily and sharply declined), education measured by any available yardstick—length of school attendance, facilities, number of teachers, taxes levied for it—has spectacularly grown over the years, over the decades, over two centuries—and so has crime. One of the few trends that matches the expansion of educational expenditures in recent decades is that multiplying incidence of crime. That does not imply a causative relationship. But it does mean that we cannot a priori assume that education necessarily results in crime reduction.

I find the example of beef and hide prices (pages 1, 8) unconvincing. We cannot produce meat without producing hides. Hides are an inescapable by-product of meat, but religious instruction is not an integral part of general education, though many parents insist justifiably that they want their children to have a religious education together with a general education. That's why we have—and should have—different types of schools, some public, some under private auspices.

It seems to me that the discourse on the Nyquist case should have been preceded by a description of the historical background—not exhaustive, but at least a discussion of the concepts and decisions leading up to it. There is a long tradition in America of connecting education and religion, going back to the "Ye Olde Deluder Satan" law of the Massachusetts Bay Colony in 1647 and the Northwest Ordinance in 1785.[b]

In *Quick Bear v. Leupp* [210 U.S. 50 (1908)] the U.S. Supreme Court

[b] "Religion, morality, and knowledge being necessary to good government and the happiness of mankind, schools and the means of education shall forever be encouraged."

found that though government is necessarily undenominational, it is not prevented by the First Amendment from purchasing education at denominational schools if the intended beneficiaries so elect.

Even when in *Everson v. Board of Education* [330 U.S. 1 (1947)] the Court restricted the use of tax funds,[c] it specifically allowed such monies to be used to reimburse parents for bus fares to send their children to a church-affiliated school. Other decisions, from *Cochran v. Board of Education* [281 U.S. 370 (1930)] to *Board of Education v. Allen* [302 U.S. 236 (1968)], sanctioned the use of tax funds for secular textbooks for children attending sectarian schools. Various federal programs made federal funds available for the benefit of pupils and students in sectarian schools— veterans' educational benefits, other forms of student aid, school lunch programs, aid for "disadvantaged" children, etc. They were never questioned. But when Pennsylvania and Rhode Island devised elaborate schemes to assist private schools while restricting expenditures of state funds in denominational schools to the teaching of secular subjects, the Court found that such controls would lead to an "excessive entanglement" between church and state and struck the programs down in *Lemon v. Kurtzman* and *Early v. Di Censo* [403 U.S. 602 (1971)].

Soon after, New York and Pennsylvania tried again, in a different form. But the Court invalidated the programs in *Committee for Public Education v. Nyquist* [413 U.S. 756 (1973)], the decision which West discusses in some detail. However, he does not mention the ringing dissents of the Chief Justice and Justices Rehnquist and White, who believe that some of or all the state programs should have been upheld. Chief Justice Burger in his dissent criticizes the contradiction within the Court's majority opinion and its neglect of what had been regarded as established doctrine in earlier decisions [413 U.S. 756 (1973) at 803]:

the statutes . . . merely attempt to equalize that 'benefit' by giving to parents of private school children, in the form of dollars or tax deductions, what the parents of public school children receive in kind. It is no more than simple equity to grant partial relief to parents who support the public schools they do not use.

In declaring state income tax deductions to parents with children in private schools to be unconstitutional—because such deductions would aid in the financing of church-affiliated schools—the Court did not consider or refer to the fact that income tax deductions are allowable for payments (donations) to churches directly and therefore patently support religious activities. The Chief Justice pointed out that the *Nyquist* decision, in overruling the District Court, runs counter to a number of earlier decisions

---

[c] Speaking through Mr. Justice Black, the Court said: "The establishment-of-religion clause of the First Amendment means at least this: . . . No tax in any amount, large or small, can be levied to support any religious activities or institutions, whatever they may be called, or whatever form they may adopt to teach or practice religion."

and particularly to the decision in *Walz v. Tax Commission* [397 U.S. 664 (1970)] in which the Court found: "The grant of a tax exemption is not sponsorship since the government does not transfer part of its revenue to churches but simply abstains from demanding that the church support the state . . ."

To be sure, the Court's majority paid no heed to these considerations in *Nyquist*. What caused Justice Powell and five other Justices to introduce a new principle which sharply contrasts with the Court's earlier decisions is pure speculation. Certainly, the New York statute authorizing tax deductions was unnecessarily complicated and ineptly drawn, which made a rejection easier. It is hard to imagine that the Court would invalidate a state statute, let alone a federal statute, which would add tuitions paid to private schools (with some inevitable restrictions) to the existing deductions for income tax purposes (including donations to churches and schools, whether church-affiliated or not). Could it be argued that a payment for tuition aids religion more directly than a donation to the same institution?

It should be mentioned that in his State of the Union Message on January 30, 1974—seven months after the *Nyquist* decision—President Nixon said:

I remain firmly committed to the principle of educational diversity. The continued health of the Nation's non-public schools is essential to this concept. Although governmental efforts aimed at supporting these schools have encountered difficulty in the courts, I believe we must continue our efforts to find ways to keep these schools open. For that reason, I continue to support legislation which permits tax credits for parents who pay to send their children to non-public schools.

It is my conclusion that West—and many others—in taking the *Nyquist* decision as the final word are unnecessarily pessimistic. A properly drawn statute, preferably federal, qualifying certain fee payments to schools, public or private, to be deductible for income tax purposes—as donations already are—if well presented, has a good chance of being upheld. A change could later be made to shift from deductions from the tax base to credits against tax liability—for tuitions, for donations and for other presently deductible items such as state and local taxes, etc.

There are signs that three of the Justices who voted on the prevailing side in the *Nyquist* case—Stewart, Blackmun, and Powell—may have second thoughts. The tone of their questions in the oral arguments on February 17, 1975, in the Pennsylvania case of *Meek v. Pittenger* (state-financed textbook loans to students in church-affiliated schools as well as special teachers, instructional equipment, and guidance and counseling) suggested a much friendlier attitude than they had shown two years earlier (April 16, 1973). Two of the Justices who can normally be relied on to vote against benefits to private schools, Douglas and Marshall, are seriously ill and may never return to the Court—at least not for very long. Their replacement could provide the necessary swing votes if a clean federal statute, not encumbered with unnecessary burdens, were to come before the Court and were persuasively presented.

It is my *conclusion*, then, that tax deductions or tax credits offer more promise in attaining the goal of aiding and reviving the ailing and declining private school education than the plan which Mr. West devised.

Response to Freeman: Tax Deduction as Aid to Parochial Schools

E.G. West

The essence of the prescriptive part (section three) of my essay was the proposal to substitute at the margin direct for indirect payments for public education. Despite the fact that Freeman explicitly states that he favors tuitions which are more nearly commensurate with the cost of instruction, he believes that my proposal is not very practicable. The main reason he argues is that of "tradition." He believes that I do not realize how much of an article of faith the present structure of public schools has become to the American public, and that I underrate the depth and strength of the tradition of *free* public schools. The "rate bills" by which school patrons paid school costs over a century ago, according to Freeman, are referred to in the current literature as examples of a bygone and benighted age. "To reintroduce them would cause an uproar that would drown out such plans."

Freeman seems to be meeting trouble halfway. It is easy to invoke "tradition" to cast doubt on the probability of *any* proposal being accepted. No doubt traditions often have useful functions. Where they do not, there is an obligation to challenge them. There are good traditions and bad traditions. The sooner the latter are opposed or brought under the light of criticism, the better. I believe that the century-old "tradition" of indirect payments instead of direct payments for education happens to be a bad one. The "tradition" of not allowing tax deductions for tuitions paid at parochial school is also a long-established one. This fact, however, does not prevent Freeman from opposing it. And I would not wish to discourage him. One of the legitimate functions of social scientists is to challenge tradition whenever necessary. It is their obligation constantly to ask de Tocqueville's question of whether what we call *necessary* institutions are simply those institutions to which we have become accustomed.

The tradition of "free" education is, in my opinion, a false one because it misinforms the public and it creates serious illusions. Moreover, its strongest supporters in the past have not been the general public (as Freeman appears to believe) but special interest groups on the supply side of education, such as teacher and administrator organizations. Of course it *is* an illusion to believe we ever had anything that can reasonably be called free education. Witness the need for most writers, including Freeman (see page 28), to place quotation marks around the word "free." The quotation marks are symbolic of the whole obscurity, ambiguity, and fiction that surrounds the subject.

Some elementary reflection and a few simple facts are all that is required to establish that no individual can escape paying for education. She or he pays, of course, through taxes of some sort or other. Table 1 quotes a recent study which estimates that as much as almost 8 percent of the income of the very poor families (those earning under $2,000 in 1960) went to education taxes. Freeman agrees with me that the poor are paying "substantial education taxes." He argues, however, that they pay them "on a uniform basis with others—which is different from having to pay a tax for sending one's children to public school." I confess that I find this part of his argument particularly difficult to understand. It is true that with *general* taxes for *general* services it is difficult to say which tax pays for which service. In the present case, however, most writers agree (including Freeman) that one can speak of *education* taxes; that is, in this case the tax source of the revenue to pay for this one particular service *can* be identified. Consider now the poorest family sending its child to a public school. We must ask the purpose of the education taxes that it is contributing. To say simply that they are contributing to "education" is unsatisfactory. One should face the question, Whose education in particular are such taxes financing? Even if the answer is that they are paying for the education of *all* children currently in the public school system, this must mean that the poor family is paying *some* fractional amount for its own child who is a member of that system. However, it is peculiar to uphold a system wherein the poorest families are contributing to the education of children from middle-class and rich homes. And if, like Freeman, we want to separate the tax-paying function from the process of consuming education, it is difficult to answer the question, Why should the rich receive free education? Moreover, even if Freeman thinks the taxes are plausibly general ones, there is nothing to stop a legislature from making them more specific or removing any vestiges of ambiguity. This degree of freedom in policy making should be significant to a legislature like New York State that seeks financial relief for private schools.

In my essay I offer one hypothesis which, I contend, is as good as any other, for an explanation of the payment of education taxes by the poorest families. Capital market imperfections can prevent many parents from drawing on their lifetime incomes in order to allow them to purchase their child's education directly. The tax system can be used to offset this deficiency by simulating such a market. The taxes, which are upon lifetime income, supply a revolving fund from which each individual draws during the period of life when his/her child is going to school. If this hypothesis is rejected, some other one must be put in its place. Freeman, however, seems reluctant to enter this field of the debate. By default he seems to be encouraging the continuation of the folk law that education is paid for by "public funds" that appear from outer space and have no connection with the individual members of society and their several motives for choosing the political process to finance their children's education. I maintain that this is another "tradition" or myth that must be challenged, and will not be challenged unless economists take the initiative. Meanwhile there is nothing to prevent governments from more precisely informing courts of law of the true and explicit purposes of their intervention. The more that a government makes clear the rationale of its educational finance, the less scope there is for the judiciary to impute its own reasoning. And the latter, as I indicated in the essay, seems at present mostly tied to the vague "public funds" doctrine.

It may indeed be, as Freeman asserts, that "current literature" refers to the "rate bills" paid directly by parents of all income groups a century ago as "examples of a bygone and benighted age." But this is the specialist literature of the modern history of education. Its authors are not representative of the average voter. Typically they come from, or are associated with, educational institutions of one kind or another that have special reasons for maintaining the status quo. We need a proper empirical test to answer the question, Does the ordinary public *really* want "free" education? One is reminded of the recent shocks to some similar conventional wisdom when the findings of an Advisory Commission on Intergovernmental Relations poll were published on the subject of who should pay for public schools. The poll revealed that the public prefers a state sales tax to a state income tax *or* a state property tax.[1] The sales tax is of course generally recognized by public finance specialists to be regressive, or certainly not progressive.

It is misleading to describe my proposal simply as one of abolishing free education. Such caricature suggests a reactionary and "antipoor" approach. The caricature itself, "abolition of free education," can of course mean many things. For example, it could mean, in Freeman's words, "tuitions which are more nearly commensurate with the cost of instruction," a situation for which Freeman himself expresses his own private preference. At another extreme, "abolition of free education" could be accomplished simply with a tiny nominal charge of say $1 per annum for public school users. My own proposal is different from either of these. I start from the empirical fact that the poorest families *are already paying* for education through various taxes. I proceed to argue initially for a switch in the type of taxation rather than a change in its magnitude. Table 2 shows that in 1960 those with a family income of $2,000 or less paid for education substantially, if indirectly, through various education taxes. My argument is that some of or all this be paid *directly*, and that a user charge is one way of accomplishing this. Of course, as the user charge is imposed, another tax—such as a property tax—is avoided. To describe this policy as one of abolishing "free" education is clearly ambiguous, for all it is doing, in effect, is making the quotation marks around the word "free" more conspicuous. Who could complain about *this*?

I contend, moreover, that the Supreme Court's interference with a government's choice of taxes would be an action that infringes on another American tradition, the tradition of the separation of powers. And if the tax modification *were* declared unconstitutional, I maintain that the correct course would be to propose to make it constitutional. Constitutional amendments in education are a common phenomenon today. They have been proposed in recent years, for instance, in the context of limiting or abolishing the property tax as the main source of revenue for education. At the same time one must not underestimate the barriers to successful amendments. There are several complexities in procedure. For instance, the constitutional amendment process in every state except Delaware requires approval by referendum. Such problems, however, are more a matter of political organization and expertise than of legal discussion around the First Amendment—the issue of central concern here.[2]

A careful consideration of the heart of my proposal will show that it is erroneous to describe it as one of "aid" to parochial schools. Rather it is a policy of avoiding hostility to them, the main thrust of the proposal being that in the future parochial school users would not be obliged to "pay twice" for their education. Freeman, on the other hand, does take up the cudgels for direct *aid* in the conventional sense. He does this mainly by persisting in his long-standing proposal for tax deductions for tuition paid at private schools, one of the types of proposals that was considered and rejected in the *Nyquist* case. He is, of course, correct to remind us that President Nixon was persuaded that this was the best approach. Indeed Freeman was one of the authorities who advised the President on the subject.[3] Nixon and other officials in the administration endorsed the enactment of a federal income tax allowance for the personal costs—tuition in particular—of private primary and secondary school attendance. The President's Commission on School Finance (the McElroy Commission) and the President's Panel on Nonpublic Education recommended them. Nixon told Catholic educators in Philadelphia in 1972 that he was "irrevocably committed" to helping nonpublic schools overcome their financial crisis.[4] The President reportedly favored a federal income tax credit of as much as $200 per child as the way to aid nonprofit private schools, which primarily means parochial schools.[5]

President Ford has also pledged his support for the Nixon policy. In a recent press conference statement he said, ". . . I think the tax credit proposed is a good proposal. The Supreme Court, unfortunately . . . declared . . . such a proposal unconstitutional. . . . I would hope that we would find some constitutional way to help private schools."[6] Nevertheless, for three successive years Congress has had bills to permit federal tax credits or exemptions for parochial school tuition, and despite an intensive lobbying effort, all three bills died in committee.

The tax deduction type of proposal clearly has political as well as legal problems to confront. It should be noticed that a tax *deduction* from income is pro-rich, for it provides a benefit that varies positively with income. Since the American income tax system is a graduated one, a benefit gives greater tax relief to a high-income tax payer than to a low-income tax payer. A $100 deduction, for example, saves $70 tax for the high-bracket taxpayer whose marginal rate reaches 70 percent, whereas it saves only $20 for the low-bracket taxpayer whose marginal tax rate climbs only to 20 percent. Those who pay no income tax obtain no benefit at all.[7]

To avoid some of this difficulty, a tax credit is often proposed instead. This gives an income-constant benefit because the creditable amount is subtracted directly from the taxpayer's bill, not from her or his income. High- and low-income tax payers get the same-size benefit as long as both have precredit liability equal to or in excess of the available credit. There is still a serious equity objection, however. The tax credit system fails to get assistance to low-income families who have little or no tax liability for the credit to offset.

It will be recalled that the *Nyquist* legislation contained three programs. Tax relief constituted one of them; the other two provided aid that would be enjoyed by the poorest families. In pushing for income tax deduction only, Freeman appears to be advocating what has been described as "middle-class legislation."[8] Social justice requires a *full tax credit scheme*, one that provides credits for indirect taxes such as sales taxes and property taxes, to which the poorest families contribute. My own proposal is equivalent to a tax credit scheme in this comprehensive sense. If everybody's tax contributions were channeled through one type of tax, the user tax, then as parents removed their children from a public school, they would obtain automatically the full "tax credit," for they would no longer be obliged to pay the user tax at that particular school. Freeman seems to be inconsistent in his approach since he argues as if indirect taxes (like sales taxes) are paid "on a uniform basis with others, which is different from having to pay a tax for sending one's children to a public school." There is obviously no relief or repeal in his system for those who do not use a public school but pay indirect taxes. Yet in the case of income tax payers, Freeman does allow such relief.

Freeman quotes the *Rodriguez* court which raised the question of whether tuition charges of public schools might unconstitutionally discriminate against the poor. He describes me as disposing "quickly" of the Court's view. I maintain that I also dispose of it accurately. The tuition charges in my plan, to repeat, are completely offset by "tax relief" in the above sense. The poor are no worse off; indeed they stand to be better off insofar as they now have more choice. My proposal does *not* discriminate against the poor. Ironically it is Freeman's that does this.

Freeman seems confident that one day his tax deduction proposal will overcome the present legal barrier that has arisen from *Nyquist* because that decision runs counter to the decision in *Walz v. Tax Commission* [397 U.S. 664 (1070)]. In that decision the Court found that the grant of a tax exemption is not sponsorship since the government simply abstains from demanding that the church support the state. But, again, if one is to rely on this kind of reasoning, one should go the whole way and allow exemption of all taxes and not simply discriminate in favor of one of them (the income tax). In the philosophy of *Walz*, if all taxes were in the form of a user tax, then the government would simply be abstaining from demanding that churchgoers support the state in the form of its public schools, when the family prefers its own church schools.

Freeman describes his proposal as providing *aid* to private schools. Implicitly there must be some reason for the state providing assistance for schooling in the first place. But this question is never raised by him. In my essay I attempt to confront this major issue. The rationale for intervention in education, which I reproduce for fresh scrutiny and to which Freeman makes no reference, is within the economist's usual schemata: the duty to protect children against potentially delinquent parents, and the obligation to internalize externalities. One can be strongly critical of some aspects of the externalities approach. (See Milton Friedman's comment in this volume and my sympathetic response to it.) Nevertheless, in trying to understand the Supreme Court's reasoning, one has to place it in this sort of framework in order to make sense of, and come to grips with, the judicial argument. I am assuming that the Court's reasoning closely corresponds to that of the conventional economist's explanation of government intervention in education. The fact that I put forward "the reduction of crime" as an example of external benefits does not mean that I personally believe that such benefits occur—only that they are often quoted in the literature and have become part of the popular folk law which no doubt the Court itself respects. I am the last person to require persuading that the evidence in fact does *not* support the argument that education reduces crime. Indeed in *Education and the State* published in 1965 I devoted a whole chapter (Chapter 4) to demonstrate this point. It is not what *I* believe about external benefits, but what others seem to believe, that I was taking as a datum. If one is not satisfied that the crime argument is representative, one can choose an alternative popularly alleged example of external benefits, e.g., that literacy is conducive to a viable exchange economy, or that it promotes economic growth.

Now, to develop the general externalities analysis in economics, one cannot avoid a joint supply model. My particular model however is misinterpreted by Freeman. He objects that religious instruction is not an integral (by-product) part of general education, whereas, in my analogy, hides are an inescapable by-product of meat. Most readers, I hope, will appreciate that my reasoning was the other way round: that general education is an inescapable by-product of religious instruction. This reasoning incidentally duplicates exactly that of the *Nyquist* court. My complaint was that they did not push it to its logical conclusion. The purchase of the general education by-product of religious instruction can logically be treated in the same way as the purchase of hides which is produced jointly with meat. The government need not be subsidizing the religious indoctrination "product" of the joint activity any more than the purchaser of hides is subsidizing the consumer of meat. This was the simple gist of my argument, and I see no reason to qualify or withdraw it. The purpose of my model was to enable those governments who wish to argue for intervention on grounds of public benefits to justify joining with private people in the finance of education. In the absence of such an argument, the Court can insist that any joint financing of parochial schools is "aid" that advances religion and causes government to become entangled with it. Without a joint supply model, Freeman is "out on a limb" in his own arguments, for, as he describes them, they are openly calculated to obtain "the goal of *aiding* and reviving the ailing and declining private school education" [my italics], a formula which could not more readily invite the hostility of the Court.

Notes

1. *Financing Schools and Property Tax Relief—A State Responsibility*, Washington, D.C., Advisory Commission on Intergovernmental Relations, January 1973, page 162.

2. Interesting and useful evidence on the question of how to proceed with constitutional amendments is contained in Donna E. Shalala, Mary F. Williams, and Andrew Fishel, *The Property Tax and the Voters*, the Institute of Philosophy and Politics of Education Teacher's College, Columbia University, Occasional Paper no. 2, November 1973.

3. R. Freeman, "Income Tax Credits for Tuition and Gifts in Nonpublic School Education," in *Tax Credits for Education* (prepared for the President's Commission on School Finance, 1971).

4. See "Tax Credits: Key Item in Latest Plan to Aid Church Schools," *U.S. News and World Report*, May 1, 1972, p. 36.

5. *New York Times*, Oct. 26, 1972, p. 1, column 8.

6. San Francisco Sunday *Examiner and Chronicle*, Oct. 13, 1974, Section A, p. 31.

7. See the excellent and informative article by John K. McNulty, "Tax Policy and Tuition Credit Legislation: Federal Income Tax Allowances or Personal Costs of Higher Education," *California Law Revue*, 61(1): January 1973.

8. Ibid., p. 10.

To West, Mostly with Love

John E. Coons

If the present Supreme Court were strongly moved by considerations of economic precision and consistency in its handling of the school aid cases, it would profit enormously from reading Professor West. He is clear, forceful, and convincing. Unfortunately, West may also be largely irrelevant. Though the present majority may be embarrassed by academic disclosures of historical and economic humbug, plainly it will be consoled by its pursuit of a holier grail—the repose of "political strife over aid to religion."[1]

On church-state issues the present Supreme Court is beset by fear of religious conflict and sectarian domination of governmental processes. Like many of their generation, the majority Justices in *Nyquist* acquired in their cradles an enduring apprehension of sacerdotal politics—a mind-set anachronistic even at that time and in ours an impediment to recognition of the authentic peril of an official ideology promoted through compulsory education. It is, at any rate, an impediment to appreciation of the Westian revelations.

Moved by its ancestral dread, the present majority has chosen in the recent school aid cases to make its contribution to civil peace by a steadfast commitment to the status quo—despise nothing old, approve nothing new, utter nothing unequivocal, and ever invoke the founding fathers. Approve tax exemptions for the bishops who own the schools,[2] yet reject the same for families who would use them, even for their secular learning. We can hope that the voters of New York will be reconciled to political impotence by imagining that Jefferson and Madison would have it so.

Whatever West's technical keenness, the political cheek of his proposals could alarm such a Court even more than the nibbling legislative efforts receiving its recent disapproval. Given its version of reality, the Court's legitimation of the most paltry user tax would initiate a permanent legislative conflict of public and private school forces—a veritable melee of monsignors and superintendents. And, once whetted, the private appetite could never be content with pecuniary placebos:

We know from long experience with both Federal and State Governments that aid programs of any kind tend to become entrenched, to escalate in cost, and to generate their own aggressive constituencies. And the larger the class of recipients, the greater the pressure for accelerated increases. . . . The potential for serious divisive political consequences needs no elaboration.[3]

Yet a possible distinction between religious politics and school politics

43

suggests itself. The Court here identifies the evil of public aid as the kindling of a legislative contest between religious and public schools for limited resources. However, the political aspects of this competition could disappear under statutory structures different from, but quite consistent with, West's purpose. Specifically, if public and private schools were subject to identical economic constraints within a general fiscal scheme, the source of political conflict would be removed. Imagine a voucher system which constituted the *exclusive* source of funding for all schools. (In the next section of this comment a program of that character will be described.) Under such a dispensation, conflict of legislative interest among school administrators would disappear, and all would stand shoulder to shoulder in the political lists. The issue would become the level of tuition support for families, not the relative share of the public pie for religious schools. Competition would be limited to the struggle for students.

The point is tempting but probably wrong. While the Court's language may suggest that the relevant conflict has featured competing school authorities, in reality public and private education often have cooperated politically as a means of stemming transfers from moribund private schools to overcrowded public schools; indeed, they had done so in the recent cases.[4] The more enduring "division" has pitted this alliance of religious and secular educators against ideological separationists who would continue to oppose all aid whatsoever. Presumably this is one form of the divisiveness that alarms the Court, and from that discord we can expect no surcease, whatever the form of aid.

Of course, if the logic of the Court's position were taken seriously, it would entail the invalidation not only of vouchers but a good chunk of the laws relating to Sunday closing, gambling, liquor control, divorce, and other areas in which religious politics are a primary feature. But that only says that here logic fails the Court. These latter statutes are constitutionally unthreatened, and the idea that religious politics bears a constitutional taint is exposed as historic and functional nonsense.[5] Perhaps the Court will ultimately resile from the application of this conceptual fancy to education; meanwhile West's effort seems largely beau geste. He must be content to inspire another, perhaps the next, generation of judges and should be evaluated more as prophet than lawyer.

So viewed, he comes off rather well. To a slightly altered Court, West's alternative proposals for user taxes would be constitutionally plausible. As he demonstrates, such systems could be legitimated even within the three-part test currently in use. Perhaps constitutional doubt could be raised concerning the secular purpose of such a dramatic shift from "free" education to positive pricing. And, presumably, one relevant effect would be an easier access to religious schools. But, whatever their present judicial prospects, models of this general sort should be presented to a refashioned majority. Ultimately its discomfort and embarrassment with the recent rendering of the First Amendment could stimulate reassessment. History suggests that a persistent public majority has a fighting chance with the most obdurate Court.[6]

West and the Poor

The user tax proposals in West's essay are too sketchy in their instrumentation to allow a clear prediction of their social consequences. This is understandable; West's purpose was to show a technical way around *Nyquist*. For this it was enough to suggest the adoption of a user tax applied either incrementally or as a substitute for the present support system of public schools. Yet West himself feels constrained to assure us briefly that the poor would not be injured.[7] It seems fair to wonder how this outcome would be guaranteed.

The problem with West's models is that user taxes in whatever amount and however progressively scaled are used for one purpose only—to limit the price effect of presently "free" public education, thereby reducing its advantage over the private sector to whatever extent public schools become dependent upon the new exactions. But how would this increase the options of low-income families? If a family with an income of $5,000 were to save $50 in user taxes by not using public schools, how much education would this buy? West's own figures show that, even if the entire present educational tax burden were returned to such families, this would fall short of the most modest full-cost private tuition.[8] (See Tables 1 and 2, pages 13 and 25.) Will West tolerate increased isolation of the "poor" in public schools, if user taxes stimulate the emigration of the middle class in large numbers?

If such an effect be disfavored, several solutions are available which are compatible with West's general aim.[a] Unfortunately all entail a greater risk than public user taxes of offending the First Amendment. They are exemplified in their most comprehensive form by the Family Choice in Education Act (FCEA), a model statute published in 1971.[8] Like West's model, the FCEA employed graduated (income) tax charges for schools; the earlier model, however, would have extended to private schools as well. Families could acquire from the state the full cost of tuition in private or public schools by making a tax payment to the state in an amount determined by the family's income and by the tuition it wished to spend.

[a] Indeed West suggests one himself in his discussion of the concept of payment from the adults' lifetime income and the loan schemes this would support (page 24). Regrettably, when applied to private tuition, it suffers from the constitutional risks attending all such voucher or loan systems.

The family, in effect, could buy education at progressively subsidized prices, an outcome which West at one point seems to approve as "economically optimal." (See page 12. I say "seems" because it is not wholly clear in this passage that West intends progressive pricing.)

The basic idea of the FCEA was suggested by the principle adopted by the Supreme Court of California in *Serrano v. Priest*,[9] that spending for a child's publicly financed education ought not be a function of wealth. The *Serrano* rule had been designed to permit school districts to enjoy spending autonomy while banning inequities associated with varying local taxable wealth. Districts would be free to spend different amounts, but only if each were "power-equalized"; that is, through any of various systems of subventions and transfers, school district budget levels would now be determined not by local wealth but by the level of locally selected tax effort. All districts would "buy" their budgets on the same tax terms.

It was observed that in such a system the geographical character of the educating unit was unimportant; any institution with wealth or income and with children to educate could be substituted. The result was "family power equalizing," embodied in the detailed provisions of the FCEA. The tax scale of the model was designed on the principle that enrollment in any school participating in the system (public or private) should trigger a tax liability which would entail "equal sacrifice" for all families using that school irrespective of their income. For example, a family with an income of $15,000 could enroll its child[b] in a high school spending $1,800 per pupil for a tax liability of $624.[10] For the same school a welfare family would pay a tax of only $15 to $25, while a wealthy family would be liable up to approximately full cost. Schools charging a wide range of tuitions could participate.

This structure was designed before either *Nyquist* or *Lemon v. Kurtzman*. It meets the social objection to the West model but only by increasing the risks from both the effect and entanglement rules. Yet there is a feature of the FCEA which conceivably could work its salvation. The majority spoke to it in *Nyquist*:

. . . we need not decide whether the significantly religious character of the statute's beneficiaries might differentiate the present case from a case involving some form of public assistance (e.g., scholarships) made available generally without regard to the sectarian-nonsectarian, or public-nonpublic nature of the institution benefitted.[11]

The Court here describes precisely the FCEA which was designed to facilitate individual choice and to be indifferent to the public or private, religious or secular character of the school selected by the family. The

---

[b] Or children; a policy decision was made to charge only one tax which would trigger the subsidy for all pupils in the family. West's position on this important point is not clear to me.

statute was plainly not intended as an aid to religion. Indeed, it could be argued that it would work to the disadvantage of the existing parochial schools.[12] However, even if the act survived the application of the purpose and effect tests, it is possible that the present Court would reject the FCEA on an entanglement rationale. The incorporation of such a protection for the poor in any user tax model could increase the odds of invalidity.[13] Yet in conscience many could not otherwise abide the social consequences.

Taming the Fractious Poor

If we scout West's proposal as perilous for the poor, along with West we should be careful to identify these potential victims. Who are the poor? I would suppose the definition of poverty to be relative to the particular commodity or service to be procured. For present purposes, poverty would mean the inability to purchase a quantity and quality of schooling sufficient to satisfy some norm—at least the compulsory education law, perhaps more. It would not be described as the status of being on welfare,[14] unless that criterion were modified to include the form of educational welfare known as the public school. This is not pejorative; of the several justifications for publicly financed education the grandest is the protection of the children of those who, unassisted, could not afford formal schooling. This justification is not discussed by West who in accounting for public financing speaks not of "poor" but only of "negligent" parents (see page 3).

To avoid understating the importance of West's enterprise, we should appreciate that the sheer numbers of the education-poor are enormous. Given the price effects of the "free" public alternative, few families can afford to pay a full-cost tuition at even the most parsimonious of private schools. Even those families now enrolled in such schools might in most cases feel constrained to desert them and to employ public education were it not for explicit and implicit private scholarships flowing from endowments, from the labor of those subject to vows of poverty, from charitable contributions, and so forth. The structure of public education finance has effectively preempted the private option for most of us.

The strength of the "price effect"—the economic inducement to choose tuition-free public schools—varies from family to family according to many factors including the following: family income; the number of school age children; special educational needs; special economic burdens (disabilities, liabilities, dependent grandparents, etc.); the level of local property tax; the level of spending (or quality) in the local public school. Finally, it varies according to the strength of the family's taste for available private education.

Note that the price effect of free provision touches all school users, a fact which distinguishes education-poverty from food- or housing-poverty where free or subsidized provision affects only a limited class of qualifying low-income families. Everyone qualifies for free education. This distinction complicates though it does not invalidate the concept of education-poverty.

This near-monopoly position has been defended as the necessary condition of a crucial externality peculiar to publicly provided education—its stated capacity to produce consensus in a nation of diverse peoples. It is only in the give and take of a tolerant and ideologically neutral public classroom that society is thought to foster adherence to organic and indispensable social norms. At one time many conceived that in the name of consensus such a public school experience must be universal. The Supreme Court frustrated this ideal in *Pierce v. Society of Sisters*,[15] but public economics has managed an approximation. At least it has successfully contained those who would constitute the principal obstacles to consensus. The rich were never likely to threaten revolution, and the parochial schools ceased to be a menace as, over time, they became less distinguishable from mediocre public schools (recently they show signs of recovering their role as a challenger of mass morality).

West's proposals, like all strategies to broaden choice, would raise anew the issue submerged in the price effects of public education. That question is not whether consensus is desirable (of course it is), nor even so much its content (though that is not without difficulty); rather it is how to achieve it, and how to achieve it without odious and stultifying compulsions that themselves impede cohesion.

Before compulsory education for the masses in public schools was imagined, the founding fathers had sought consensus; and they supposed that, for their own time, they had achieved all the consensus they needed in securing adoption of the Bill of Rights. For future generations the problem would be the maintenance of an informed and motivated public that would support those rights. Thus, the original version of the national compact was simply this: Americans agree and must continue to agree that no orthodoxy be given official approval. Madison and Jefferson repeatedly described the ideal polity as an unrestrained competition of ideas.[16] For them, the familiar villain in those preindustrial, preimmigrant, preurban days was the intolerant theological state; this view was reflected in the drafting of the First Amendment.

The counterpart to that villain in our time is painfully plain. At the risk of mimicking the *Nyquist* majority, suppose that Jefferson were confronted with the modern public school which only the rich and Catholics can afford to escape. Would he perhaps grieve that the First Amendment reads "religion" instead of "ideology"? Could he distinguish an establishment of one from the other? Even the present Court has found their distinction tenuous in other contexts, for example, in the case of conscientious objection by nonbelievers.[17] It may find it increasingly difficult in compulsory education.

Note that the complaint here is not about indoctrination which, after all, is the lot of all involuntary students, public and private. All teaching—"neutrality" included—is value-laden. Nor is the problem the particular value content of public school indoctrination; I will assume that it is sound and good. The problem is compulsion; for all but the rich public school is an inescapable official philosophy. Conceivably the imposition of this system of approved thought will become unconstitutional in our time, though I doubt it.[18] In any event it is a reproach to the values that inform the First Amendment.

This is not to make light of the traditional church-state problem, but only to remind that there are establishments and establishments. One would hope that the Court would become wary of ideological monoliths irrespective of their secular, religious, or humanistic credentials. Given a more balanced sensitivity, the Court might perceive anti-establishment— even Jeffersonian—virtues in such laws as it has latterly slaughtered.

Public educators have long assumed that coercive clustering of nonrich families to learn the American way would have the centripetal outcome desired. If ever this view of consensus were empirically obvious, it is no longer. Indeed, the opposite is equally plausible—that, in restraining the states from supporting the educational and ideological notions of individual citizens, the Court itself commits the quintessential act of divisiveness. Consensus in the end may be reserved for those societies that manifest trust in the private preferences of their members. Such societies are commonly called pluralistic.

West and the Children

This comment cannot do justice to the many and important issues arising from the natural and legal subordinations of children. (Fortunately Sugarman has addressed some of these questions; see pages 74-75.) I would only note the paradox that coercive indoctrination of the children of the nonrich in public schools could be defended on civil libertarian grounds. Children—at least young children—are the inevitable subjects of domination by adults. The only question is who will dominate them in a manner which will best serve their present interest and advance their eventual autonomy. It is at least open to argument that the state best achieves this end by excluding parental influence. Ironically, increasing family choice can be described as the ultimate form of ideological imposition upon children—subjection to the arbitrary whim of individual parents. In this view it is the children of the nonrich who now enjoy the greatest freedom and fulfillment in education, for it is they alone who are delivered from the risk of being forced by their parents to attend private school. Vouchers would foreclose the child of the poor from the highroad to personal autonomy represented in the guarantee of a public education.

This seems to me a plausible argument; even if it is principally false (as it is), it suggests some important truths. One is that the state must remain prepared, when necessary, to paternalize and to interfere with the family, as it must with any institution holding the capacity to oppress. The state must protect children with guarantees of physical integrity and of adequate minimums in education. The fraternity of thoughtful conservatives like West who have promoted parental choice in the name of liberty must at some point come to grips with the fundamental criticism that parental control is tyranny. They have apparently assumed that where families are adequately supported, a rather broad control by parents or parental substitutes is about as close to meaningful liberty as political art can contrive. That assumption may represent common sense in the case of small children, but the rationale is as yet wholly wanting. And, for older children, unlimited parental hegemony is problematic on its face. High school vouchers, for example, would counsel a regime more sensitive to the user's own preference—at least in the form of a veto on selection of school. As long as it fails to distinguish the interest of child and parent, the libertarian case remains unfinished. However, I concede that where mechanisms of choice require a cash payment, giving the voucher to the pupil presents interesting and difficult questions.

Notes

1. *Committee for Public Education and Religion Liberty v. Nyquist*, 413 U.S. 756, 794 (1973). See also *Sloan v. Lemon*, 413 U.S. 825 (1973); *Lemon v. Kurtzman*, 403 U.S. 602, 622 (1971).

2. Indeed, for their houses of worship. See *Walz v. Tax Commission*, 394 U.S. 664 (1970).

3. 413 U.S. at 797. The Court apparently has concluded that a flat proscription of aid will eliminate divisive political consequences. How it would accommodate retaliatory opposition to public school tax referenda in the scheme of things is unclear.

4. One of the justifications pressed upon the Court in *Nyquist* was the secular purpose and effect of assisting the public schools. 413 U.S. at 765, 773, 783.

5. See Choper, "The Establishment Clause and Aid to Parochial Schools," 56 *U. Cal. L. R.* 260, 273 (1968).

6. Indeed, in the long run the legitimation of artfully designed user taxes may be threatened less by the federal Constitution than by the guarantees of a "free" education in a number of key state constitutions. See, e.g., *N.Y. Const.*, Art. XI, §1; *Conn. Const.*, Art. VIII, §1; *N.J. Const.*, Art. VII, §4; *Pa. Const.*, Art X, §1. The super majority ordinarily required for constitutional amendment would not easily be mustered. In fact, any majority for tuition in public schools might come hard.

7. See West (this book), at p. 24.

8. J. Coons and S. Sugarman, *Family Choice in Education: A Model State System for Vouchers*, Institute of Government Studies (Berkeley, 1971). And see generally Center for Study of Public Policy, *Educational Vouchers* (Cambridge, 1970); G. LaNone.

9. 5 Cal. 3d 584, 487 P.2d 1241 (1971).

10. See Coons and Sugarman, op. cit., note 10, at pp. 61, 65, 77-78.

11. 413 U.S. at 782.

12. See Coons and Sugarman, op. cit., note 10, at p. 20.

13. But see the hopeful analysis of this issue in Sugarman, "Family Choice: The Next Step in the Quest for Equal Educational Opportunity?" 38 *L. and Contemp. Prob.* 513, 529-530 (1974).

14. See, e.g., Note, "A Statistical Analysis of the School Finance Decisions: On Winning Battles and Losing Wars," 81 *Yale L. J.* 1303 (1972).

15. 268 U.S. 510 (1925).

16. Madison's specific hope was that American society ". . . itself will be broken into so many parts, interests, and classes of citizens, that the right of individuals, or of the minority, will be in little danger from interested combinations of the majority." *The Federalist, No. 51*. For examples of Jefferson's views, see his *Notes on Virginia*, Query 17.

17. *Gillette v. United States*, 401 U.S. 437 (1971); *Welsh v. United States*, 398 U.S. 333 (1970); *United States v. Seeger*, 380 U.S. 163 (1965).

18. Certainly the Chief Justice would like to confine such omens as *Wisconsin v. Yoder* [406 U.S. 205, 235 (1972)] to historic (and minuscule) religious dissent. However, the more he distinguishes the Amish from other ideological dissenters, the less I understand the difference.

Response to Coons: Liberty, Equality, and Expediency

E.G. West

The subject under discussion, like most others in the realms of social organization, can be approached from two directions: what economists call positive and normative treatments. The positive treatment is more "hard-nosed" in that it does not preach ideal solutions to virtuous people within an unrealistically "perfect" system, but rather seeks to explain and to predict actual (expedient) outcomes in a real-world "imperfect" setting. The normative approach, on the other hand, deals with what the authors themselves think *ought* to happen. It attempts to prescribe policy on the assumption of previously accepted values, or values that the author himself elevates to positions of dominating importance. Both the positive and the normative approaches are evident in Coons's contribution to the discussion. The intention of my initial piece was largely an essay in positive economics. For this reason, much of Coons's normative critique is irrelevant to my first essay. I shall allow myself, however, to enter into normative discussion here because it may place some of the debate into better perspective. (See also my second essay at the end of this book, an essay that was largely prodded into life by John Coons's present piece.) Moreover, doing this at Coons's provocation is likely to provide particular stimulus. I intend to devote most of this response to the normative issues raised. To bring us back to my main argument, I shall return to emphasize its "positive" nature in the last few paragraphs.

Before assessing a system on the basis of value judgments, the values themselves must be clearly enumerated. In American education the two most important values are liberty and equality. The writing of the First Amendment was clearly influenced by the desire for liberty, in this case, liberty of religion. Try as he may, Coons cannot conceal that on this issue he sits firmly on the right hand of the founding fathers. Yet curiously he seems intent on giving the impression that "equality" is what he *really* and mainly wants, and he elects with gusto to judge my essay accordingly. The equality debate, of course, is a tricky one. Coons's particular contribution can be playfully described as "A Pilgrim's Progress through the Slough of Distribution." One can more easily progress, of course, by asserting that one's concern for the poor is more intense than the other fellow's. If I didn't know him better, I would have suspected some "holier than thou-ness" to begin to show itself where Coons argues that my proposals are "too sketchy in their instrumentation to allow a clear prediction of their social consequences." He fills the gap by grafting onto the whole discussion what, in his mind, *is* a clear prediction—that the result of my proposal *will* be injurious to the poor. He asks initially whether I will tolerate increased isolation of the poor in public schools *if* user taxes stimulate the emigration of the middle class in large numbers. The tone of the discussion then proceeds as if the conjunction *if* had been forgotten or replaced with *when*.

I shall say more on the accuracy of this "prediction" later. It is instructive first to assume that my proposals will indeed increase inequality. Since the argument is still in the realm of value judgments, a normative case against my proposal is not yet established. The matter must still be resolved by a choice or trade-off between values. Are we more egalitarian than libertarian? The feeling for liberty may be so intense that society may wish to opt for this value even at the cost of some increased inequality. This is likely to be more so if the "equality" in a public system is arrived at by way of leveling down. Expressed the other way round, innovation that grants more liberty may be acceptable if at least the person in the lowest income level obtains some benefit even though this is *relatively* less than the benefits enjoyed by people above her or him.[1] Those who argue that granting free choice will stimulate competition and thereby improve all schools could argue that absolute benefits *could* accrue to all school patrons whatever their income group.

To come now to questions of concrete predictions concerning the outcome of my proposals. One must be careful not to fall into the trap of comparing these with some ideal or utopian system and then describing any discrepancy as a measure of failure or inefficiency. The comparison should be with the present educational system as it actually stands. Those like Coons whose most vocal complaint is that the present educational system is grossly unequal must remember that this is the starting point for reform. Put in its strongest terms, therefore, his query is whether my proposals would make the outcome any worse that it is already. In this perspective I cannot see that Coons's argument about the social consequences of my proposals really succeeds.

What now of the accuracy of his prediction? On the question of a poor family's purchasing potential for private schooling after receiving full tax relief, he seems seriously to be misinterpreting my evidence. He argues that even if the entire present educational tax burden were returned to poor families, this would fall short of the most modest full cost to private tuition. The figures I used on this issue were those provided by Coons's colleague Grubb in a cost benefit study of education relating to the year 1960. Table 2, which is based on Grubb's figures, shows the absolute amounts that were paid in that year by different family income groups. The median income that year was around $7,000. I shall assume that a family that is defined as poor will never attain the median income even for a short period *at any time in its lifetime*. Consider, therefore, a family with a lifetime cycle of say 50 years. Assume that the head of the family works for 10 years in each of the first five income earning categories in Table 2.[a] In its first 10 years, the family will be in the income group earning up to $2,000; in the second 10 years, it will earn $2,000 to $2,999; and so on. In its last 10 years, it attains the category of $5,000 to $5,999, which is still below the median. On this basis, the total *undiscounted* lifetime contributions in education taxes of this poor family will amount to $7,380. Assume for the moment that the family has one child to educate and that the education lasts for 10 years. Ignoring temporarily the problem of discounting (or assume the rate of interest is zero), a rebate of lifetime tax contributions would provide it with $738 per annum, or $92 per month, where education takes place for eight months of the year. We have to bear in mind that the drop-out rate is highest in the lowest-income groups; or, in other words, the higher-income groups get a bigger duration of education for their tax dollar.[2] If the poor family's child has an education that lasts only 8 years, then a full tax rebate would provide the family with $115 per month to purchase the equivalent amount.

Next, we have to take account of the fact that since 1960, the year of the data, there has been inflation. Assuming an average annual inflation rate of 5 percent, and assuming that the structure of taxation has not altered significantly, we must approximately double our figures. Thus our poor family in 1975 would have $184 per month available for a 10-year education and $230 for an 8-year education. Of course, if there are two children in the family, these figures have to be halved; if there are three children, they have to be divided by three; and so on. The Fleischmann report on New York education estimated that in 1970 total tuition and operating costs per pupil at Catholic elementary schools amounted to $244 per year.[3] Cost increases and inflation will have since increased this figure. If we mark up the figure reasonably by 50 percent, we arrive at $366 total cost per annum per pupil in Catholic elementary schools, or about $46 per month (assuming an 8-month educational year). On these figures our poor family would be able to purchase an education for two children at such parochial schools.

We next have to allow, realistically, for discounting; that is, we must assume that the rate of interest is positive. A family that draws on *future* tax contributions should receive something less than those contributions according to the interest rate charge on the "advance." At the same time, *past* tax contributions by the adult members of the family will yield larger amounts when they draw on them because they have been "earning" interest (i.e., they need to be *compounded* forward). Consider a couple that marries when each partner is 25 years old. Assume that both have been earning for 10 years and paying education taxes. Property tax burden could have been felt through "shifting the incidence" in the form of expensive

---

[a] The typical poor family is not likely to remain in the $2,000 column throughout its life. In other words, poor families progress through different income groups as the family head gets older.

house rentals. Other indirect taxes such as sales taxes are also incurred and are destined for education budgets. Suppose this family has its first child when the parents are 26 years old. The child will be ready for public school six years later when the parents are 32 years old. They will have been paying educational taxes for 17 years when their first child goes to school. Assume that during the next 15 years the family is paying taxes and educating children, i.e., up to a parental age of 47 years. From 47 years to 70 years (i.e., another 23 years) the adults pay further taxes even though their children have left home. It can now be seen that while there is a need to discount the family "advance" on the taxes paid in the last 23 years, this is offset considerably by the compounding necessary with respect to the first 17 years of tax payments before the children reached school. The result is that typically *some* net discounting is necessary, but it is not as substantial as might be imagined at first. I would estimate roughly that the family would have at least $150 available per month for a 10-year education and at least $190 for an 8-year one.

All this strongly indicates that *a large section of the poor* would be able to finance the equivalent duration of education in parochial schools if they received a tax rebate. This does not deny that *some* individuals within the group classified as "poor" would not be able to meet *all* the costs of their children's education. Nevertheless the findings are surely significant. *Even the poorest of the poor would be able to finance a substantial percentage of the full cost of their children's education.* In the proper context of my discussion, these findings are of the highest importance.[4] The clientele of parochial schools in New York State include large numbers of the very poorest. If they received a full tax rebate (or were exempted taxation in the first place), they would be in a position to pay much more than the tuition charges they are presently paying since the parochial system itself allocates its own private subsidies to the poorest. In opposing full tax rebates, Coons is defending a system which is itself largely antipoor in these respects.

It will be recalled that my introduction of the user tax was not initially intended to substitute all other taxes. The immediate purpose was to complement them at the margin in order to finance future increases in cost. It is in this context that we should consider Coons's question: "If a family with an income of $5,000 could save $50 in user taxes by not using a public school, how much education would this buy?" The point of my argument here is that if such a scheme were implemented, the present parochial schools would at least have a chance of maintaining themselves in their present numbers if they could receive some *marginal* relief. If costs go up in one year by $50 and a parent is asked to pay most of this sum to a public system, but only as a user charge at his customary parochial schools, the chances of the school surviving increase dramatically. Moreover, choice will also increase significantly.

One must not characterize Coons as being resigned to the public system in its present form. As he reminds us, he has produced, in collaboration with his colleague Sugarman (another contributor to this symposium), an attempt to reshape the present public system to achieve more equality.[5] It will be useful here to give more account of this previous work and also of another important volume of which Coons was a coauthor: *Private Wealth and Public Education*, 1970, by John E. Coons, William H. Clune, and Stephen B. Sugarman. A scrutiny of these previous writings, I believe, will give more insight into the normative dilemmas involved, dilemmas which are perhaps not fully appreciated by Coons and his colleagues.

Their 1970 volume points out that there has been pressure for reform since the beginning of this century, inspired with the aim of reducing substantial inequalities in the raising of educational revenues and in the distribution of educational resources in nearly every state in America. The main initiative, they observe, has largely been administrative and academic. Efforts for reform through litigation did not get under way until the late 1960s. The first real victory came with the California Supreme Court's judgment in *Serrano v. Priest* in 1971. The court put forward a negative constitutional principle that the quality of public education may not be "a function of the wealth of ... (a pupil's) parents and neighbors." It is this so-called principle of "fiscal neutrality" that is the central policy aim of the 1970 book. (Indeed it is believed that the particular arguments in their book had a direct influence on the recent judicial decisions.) The authors argue that a fiscal neutrality that is consistent with the 14th Amendment should not involve the court in the intricacies of particular expenditure patterns or quantities. Accordingly, they devise what to them is the simple rule of "district power equalizing" (DPE). By this they mean a system whereby equal tax rates among districts should provide equal spendable dollars. The local unit would be empowered to fix the tax rate (effort) to be imposed upon a specific class of local wealth. For every level of local tax effort permitted by statute, the state would have fixed the number of dollars per task unit (e.g., per pupil) that the district would be empowered to spend.

Imagine, for instance, a state divided into two school districts A and B. Each has 100 pupils. District A has a total wealth of $10,000 ($100 pupils). District B has a total of $90,000, or $900 per pupil. Each decides to tax its wealth at the rate of 10 percent for schools, yielding $10 and $90 per pupil respectively. In this case the authors would regard district A as being $80 short. But since it tried just as hard as the richer district (10 percent tax on wealth in each case), it should be able to buy just as good a school. The $80 is to come from a state tax. The total wealth of the state is $100,000; so in order to raise the $80 per pupil for district A, the state chooses to levy a flat 8 percent tax, producing $72 per pupil from district B and $8 from district A. In the end district A pays $10 local tax plus $8 state tax, or $18 total. District

B pays $90 local plus $72 state, or $162 total. As a percentage of local wealth, each total tax is exactly the same, while the redistribution of wealth has produced equal expenditures. Each is taxed at 10 percent locally and 18 percent totally, and each has $90 to spend.

The Coons, Clune, and Sugarman model is accompanied by explicitly normative analysis in support. The supreme virtue of their system, they claim, is that it harmonizes two important values in American society, equality and "subsidiarity." The latter term encompasses the idea of local autonomy. They emphasise that complete autonomy implies at least the power of localities to decide (1) how much education they desire, and (2) how much they are willing to spend to reach their goals. They are resigned to the fact that some localities will spend more than others and that some degree of inequality in this sense will result. Thus in the above example, A could tax itself only 5 percent—in which case B would spend twice as much per pupil as A. Clearly this system is subject to the same criticism that Coons leveled against mine—that there is no clear prediction of the social consequences. This is even more true in the FCEA model because it involves a cessation of local property tax, and a vague reference to a "funding of the total system . . . based primarily on statewide sources."[6] Although the authors give hints that they would prefer a state wealth tax or a state progressive income tax, they leave us considerably in the dark. If left to the "political process" to decide (as they also seem to suggest in some places), some outcomes could completely pervert their quest for equality. A recent Advisory Commission on Intergovernmental Relations poll on the subject of who should pay for the public schools revealed that the public prefers a state sales tax to a state income or state property tax.[7] The sales tax, of course, is generally regarded as the most regressive of all.

Coons, Clune, and Sugarman emphasize that no way has yet been perceived to "harmonize subsidiarity and equal opportunity"; they oppose the conventional administrative prescription for the curing of severe inequalities—complete centralization and uniformity of fiscal policy. They reject this because it would almost completely erode local autonomy (subsidiarity). Theirs then, in their own description, is a policy of balance or tension between two values, a balance that they believe to suit particularly the needs and traditions of America. Clearly Coons's own philosophy does not support "equality" as the value absolute. Otherwise there would be no need to stress the need for a "balance." And his equality is being balanced in effect with liberty. For "subsidiarity," meaning full diffusion and dispersion of decision making, including the decision of individuals to choose parochial schools, means just that.

The authors anticipate, in passing, the criticism that the DPE proposal exaggerates the difference that money makes: "If in fact dollars for schools

have no positive effect, . . . this book is largely a sterile exercise."
Obviously some reaction had to be given to the Coleman report of the late
1960s which did in fact cast doubt on the traditional belief that per-pupil
expenditures showed direct relation to achievement when social
background and attitudes of individual students and their classmates were
held constant. Coons and his coauthors were obviously not too disturbed
about the new uncertainties of this evidence. They argue that if money is
indeed inadequate to improve education, "the residents of poor districts
would at least have an equal opportunity to be disappointed by its failure."

Interestingly enough, their 1970 book carries a foreword by the "ar-
chitect" of the Coleman report himself. In it Coleman emphasizes strongly
that one must always ask of any method of public finance what incentives it
creates or destroys, and what the consequences of these incentives might
be. One disadvantage Coleman attributes to the "power-equalizing"
scheme is the incentive for the well-to-do family to move its children from
public school to private school since even by voting high local school taxes,
the benefits of these taxes would be low in a wealthy community. Yet he
acknowledges that power equalizing provides a less extreme incentive for
rich parents to withdraw from the public system than would a fully central-
ized system that equalized educational wealth and effort across a state. It
seems odd that, anxious as Coleman is to test for the incentives of any
scheme, he does not apply the same test (of incentives) to the very public
system of "free education" that he wants to preserve intact at all cost. The
two main criteria for reward for the teaching personnel within that system
are (1) the education of the teacher (the number of his/her diplomas etc.)
and (2) the experience of the teacher (the number of years service). The
effort of the teacher is thus not geared to his diligence in the classroom and
is thus not directed toward satisfying the wishes of the direct consumer, the
family, or the parent. This is obviously a severe constrant on efficiency. It
has led some writers[8] to predict that the distribution of industrious and
good teaching will be as random as the charitable impulses among the
teaching profession; and this hypothesis seems to explain well the disturbing evidence of Coleman's own research to the effect that educational
achievement and effectiveness were also distributed randomly.

Coons, Clune, and Sugarman seem to reveal no such inhibitions as does
Coleman, for they boldly acknowledge that the time is due for a return of
some market discipline into education. Following this up in their 1971 study
(FCEA, p. 334), Coons and Sugarman would also allow public schools that
could not maintain enrollment to go bankrupt. And the three 1970 authors
are quite anxious to push their notion of subsidiarity to the level of freedom
of family choice. Indeed they explicitly acknowledge that their *district*
power equalizing solution translates freely into a *family* power equalizing
solution. This leads them to an interesting and sympathetic discussion of

Friedman's voucher system. Ultimately, however, the freedom of choice implied in the latter is not sufficient for them; the parent must also be given some choice in the setting of the particular financial level of expenditure (voucher). Now a situation of nonintervention where the parents purchase education for their children just as they do food, clothing, and accommodation, does just this; and the parent does not have to go through a clumsy and expensive political process to do it. The authors are prevented from going *this* far however. The chief impediment appears to be arguments and evidence (that they have accepted from historians) that too many parents would be too poor, and some too irresponsible to do justice to the child. My first response to this is that my own historical researches produce different results.[9] Second, compulsory laws can in any case take care of much of the irresponsibility problem. My third response is that the problem of financial inability seems to me not to have been clearly demonstrated—witness the above estimates of lifetime tax contributions toward education of the poorest families. Fourth, in those instances where relevant poverty *is* demonstrated for a small minority, the best solution is surely by way of simple fiscal transfer.

In focusing on inequality of tax revenue allocation to *public* education, Coons, Clune, and Sugarman have been somewhat off target. The lack of "fair shares" expresses itself more seriously in unfair share of choices available. The rich are much more mobile within the present public system and are therefore able to settle at the most efficient points within it. The poor are less able to move and to choose. The point was made by Charles Benson in his introduction to FCEA: "The rich can afford private education, and the private sector offers substantially greater diversity among institutions than does the public sector. Some of those who cannot afford private education can obtain access to a different school by moving their residence. This may be a high price, and in any event, there is not much diversity by type of institution within the public sector. The poor who cannot move have no choice."[10] Coons and Sugarman themselves justify their scheme for increased choice on the grounds of the need "to purge public education of discrimination against . . . poor people."[11] My argument is that returning the poor families' tax money through, for instance, a loan system at the lower education level is surely the most efficient way of reinstating *meaningful choice* and therefore of achieving the authors' objective—desire for a change toward equality of opportunity that really *is* consistent with "subsidiarity." It is in this way that I believe that the pursuits of increased liberty and equality are more likely to be complementary than competitive goals in my proposals.

If choice is to mean anything, it means a choice between *all* alternatives. The choice that is incorporated into the FCEA is a constrained one. The money to supply education is first taken from the poor as from everybody else, and is then redistributed to them through the political process. As it is redistributed, it falls into the category of "aid." This results in two major constraints: First it gives the state the right to incorporate all kinds of conditions that confine free choice, and, incidentally, because they need policing, involve heavy extra expenditure in inspection and bureaucracy. Second, since people's own money is filtered through *government* channels into forms of "aid," selection of parochial schools is severely curtailed because the First Amendment problem is invoked. Indeed, in an attempt to acknowledge this, the FCEA incorporates limitations on grants to parochial schools. The religious school can receive only 90 percent of the public dollars available to secular private schools. All state spending, moreover, is conditioned upon the schools devoting at least three-quarters of expenditure to secular instruction, and at least 4 hours of secular instruction is required daily. Obviously Coons and Sugarman are not treating the issue of parochial education as a joint supply problem as I do; their analysis is implicitly based on the separate supply assumption (e.g., religion at one part of the day and curriculum and secular instruction at another). For reasons expressed at length in my opening essay, the only logical way of rationalizing the partnership of government in the education that takes place in parochial schools, and in such a way that does not violate the First Amendment, is by use of the joint supply model—which is closer to reality. In calling for separate accounting for religion and secular instruction, the FCEA runs into all the difficulties that were experienced by New York State in implementing separate accounting proposals. Coons admits that it is possible that the present Court would reject the FCEA on entanglement grounds. In my opinion there is little doubt at all that the entanglement issue would be a complete barrier.

While in my own essay I argued that the logical rationale of state participation with parochial schools necessitated the joint supply model, I was not sanguine about the hopes of the Court's accepting it. For this reason, my argument eventually concentrated upon the protection given to parochial schools by the Free Exercise clause in the First Amendment. To do this, my scheme focused upon avoiding, as much as possible, the filtering of individual's (including the poorest individual's)monetary payment for education through the political process in the first place. $200 spent by a poor family on education taxes and then dispatched to it as a voucher spendable in a parochial school would most probably be regarded as infringing on the First Amendment because the Court will see it as "aid" from "public funds." The same $200 spent by the same poor family directly on parochial schooling would *not* infringe on the Establishment clause, and any restrictions on such spending that were attempted would probably be regarded as infringing on the Free Exercise clause. In this way, choice is not constrained, and the problem about the Establishment Clause is avoided. The only potential objection that I can imagine Coons entertaining is contained in his words: "In conscience many could not abide the social consequences." This has nothing to do with the First Amendment. Moreover, I maintain that in any case even the social consequences would be to Coons's liking, for the competition that is encouraged by the direct method of purchase of any service tends to keep the costs of that service lowest. My proposal gives the poor this "weapon" whereas, as Charles Benson agrees, only the rich now have it. Coons's proposal does not provide the same weapon, and it is *his* proposals that lead to social consequences that are uncertain. Moreover, if he can prove that his system does accomplish redistribution toward the poor, this can be matched in my system simply by a restructured general tax system, a system that would include such policies as a guaranteed minimum income or a negative income tax. I personally doubt that the Coons's system would involve redistribution to the poor. In fact, it is more likely to make them worse off. There are strong reasons to believe that a democracy that is based on simple majority voting and therefore gives special weight to the preferences of the middle voter is likely to involve redistribution from both the rich and the poor parts of the population in favor of that same middle voter. But here we encounter the actual political world, a world in which the personal value judgments or preferences of either Coons or myself are not likely to count for much. It is for this reason that I consider the positive economic approach more relevant to real world solutions.

Positive Economics

In the third section of my essay I started with the assumption that the median (middle) voters already possess capital value in their strategic position, a value that accrues from various redistributional benefits that they enjoy. One of these benefits is the enjoyment of publicly provided "free" schools that are subsidized by many who opt for parochial or private schools and thus have to pay twice. A threat to this benefit occurs when their "benefactors," the parochial school users, begin to be forced into public schools where they only pay once. This happens when there is an increasing likelihood that the private schools will go bankrupt through dramatically increasing costs. The solution sought is one which would best meet the self-interest of the key voters (whether or not Coons or I like it). I assume that the threatened incursions on the benefits of the middle voters come mainly in the form of higher taxes and/or less efficient education for their children caused by classrooms that are crowded with "parochial school refugees." There is some minimum price that they will pay to avoid this outcome. Testimony to the fact that this attitude prevails is given in the willingness of the New York State government to grant marginal and modest aid to the ailing parochial schools. The problem is how to achieve the *same degree* of financial relief in a manner that does not infringe on the First Amendment. My argument is that the *marginal* user taxes provide one such escape route. It is a route by which all parties are benefited, or, in the terms of economics, it is the move that is "Pareto optimal." The Coons plan for education does not achieve this mutual benefit, and it is unlikely therefore to stem the destruction of parochial schools. His plan is politically ambitious, and the middle voters are not likely to support it because, due to the considerable uncertainty as to outcome, they will fear even further losses of benefits.

One remaining point intrigues me as a nonlawyer. Coons indicates that a modest and marginal user tax would itself have to face judicial scrutiny. I would welcome further instruction on this. I had always believed that the type of taxation that a government decided upon was a matter for the government alone according to the American doctrine of the Separation of Powers. Perhaps Coons's argument is that the user tax would be looked upon as a fee and would therefore fail to pass muster in those states in which the constitution had decreed "free" public education. My reply here would be to debate legally the meaning of "free" with or without quotation marks. If necessary, I would then argue for a constitutional amendment. In those many cases where state government did *not* decree "free" education in their constitutions, I believe that my user tax proposal would stand a good chance of surviving judicial scrutiny. First, a court could not object that low-income groups could not afford the new user tax if that tax replaces, and is no bigger than, the alternative tax that the poor are already paying or would pay in the future. Second, the child is protected against receiving a deficient education because compulsory education laws are on the statute. Third, bearing in mind that the present system is antipoor insofar as there are many poor children attending parochial schools and therefore double payment for education is involved, the new switch to user taxes would remove this inequity. In New York State, the area that my essay focused upon, it is important to notice that the average income of the parochial school families is less than the median income for the state as a whole. Fourth, if further income redistribution in favor of the poor was required, this could be met by a simultaneous policy of redistribution via alternative fiscal means. Concern for the poor does not prevent a continuation of a flat price system in other public services, such as the post office, public transit, road construction, and metered public parking. Fifth, even if the above arguments were still not cogent enough, a case for not charging the poor for education does not apply to the vast (and growing) majority of families who are not poor. The note in *Rodriguez* certainly intimated that a tuition charge at a public school might unconstitutionally discriminate against the poor if it had the effect of excluding them from minimum of public education. But this posture by the Court excludes it from any concern about the majority of families, that is, the nonpoor; these presumably could face the user tax without hazard, and insofar as they do, the tax relief to parochial schools is still significant and effective.

Notes

1. This would seem to be in line with Rawls's "Difference Principle." See John Rawls, *A Theory of Justice*, Harvard, Cambridge, 1971, page 65. Notice that I am assuming that liberty and equality are competitive norms; but this only for the sake of argument. My own proposals, I believe, are consistent with a view of liberty and equality being complementary, rather than competitive.

2. A recent study has shown that there is also a considerable variance in the number of hours taught per year in American schools. D. E. Wiley and A. Harnischfeger, "Quantity of Schooling and Exposure to Instruction," *Education Research*, 3(4): April 1974.

3. *New York State Commission on the Quality, Cost and Financing of Elementary and Secondary Education*, 1972, Vol. 1, Table 5.5.

4. Ibid.

5. J. Coons and S. Sugarman, *Family Choice in Education: A Model State System for Vouchers*, Institute of Government Studies (Berkeley, 1971), hereafter referred to as FCEA (an abbreviation for Family Choice in Education Act).

6. Ibid., page 334.

7. *Financing Schools and Property Tax Relief–A State Responsibility*, Washington, D.C., Advisory Commission on Intergovernmental Relations, January 1973, page 162.

8. Winston C. Bush, Alan Freiden, and Robert Staaf, "Of the Expense of the Institutions for the Education of Youth: Adam Smith Revisited." Private Monograph, Virginia Polytechnic Institute, Blacksburg, Virginia.

9. On the general case see E. G. West, *Education and the Industrial Revolution*, Gage, Ontario, 1975. Also on the case of New York State in particular see: "The Political Economy of American Public School Legislation," *Journal of Law and Economics*, Vol. 10, 1967, pp. 101-124.

10. FCEA, page 324.

11. FCEA, page 327.

New Perspectives on "Aid" to Private School Users

Stephen D. Sugarman

West's analysis of state aid to religious schools provides us with another stimulating addition to the literature of education, economics, and law; in view of his earlier work, it comes as no surprise that he is led to recommend charging for education instead of our present scheme in which state education is tuitionfree.[1] Yet his economic analysis of the United States Supreme Court's approach to the Establishment clause and his recommendations and predictions regarding future laws in aid of nonpublic school users are refreshing; I will direct my comments toward both these sets of observations.

What Constitutes a "Law Respecting an Establishment of Religion"?

The joint supply model which West employs provides a helpful analogy through which the Supreme Court's treatment of the Establishment clause in the "aid to religion" cases may be examined. The basic point of the model and analogy is that, because of the interdependency of beef (education) and hides (religion), if what society wants is beef consumption (education) and it intervenes in the market to stimulate the production or purchase of cattle, this intervention will necessarily benefit the consumers of hides (religion). Viewed in this light, the line drawing in which the Court has engaged seems rather odd to West. The Court has, by analogy, upheld schemes by which the government (1) pays for the transport of cattle to market,[2] (2) provides feed for the cattle to eat,[3] and (3) exempts from taxes that land which is used for the raising of animals.[4] Following the analogy, it also appears to be constitutional to provide ordinary municipal services to cattle producers[5] and to grant tax deductions to those who donate money to nonprofit animal farms.[a] On the other hand, the Court has struck down plans which, by analogy, (1) provide money directly to cattle producers, even if earmarked for cleaning the cattle pens,[6] and (2) provide money—refunds—to buyers based upon their purchases of cattle.[7] To West these seem to be distinctions without meaningful differences, as there is a beneficial impact on users of hides in every case. This criticism of the Court's

---

[a]The Supreme Court has not actually passed on the constitutionality of Section 17C of the Internal Revenue Code which allows taxpayers deductions for contributions to charitable organizations including religious organizations.

decisions is not novel, although the economics of legal commentators who have talked of each of the schemes as "freeing funds" for religion (i.e., benefiting hides) may be less elegant.[8]

Finding these differing state programs not distinguishable in terms of their basic economic effects still leaves us with the question of how they should all come out. West uses the joint supply model seemingly to suggest where he thinks the line of constitutionality should be drawn in these "aid to religion" cases. The argument has two steps: first, what ought to be seen to offend the Establishment clause is the subsidy of religion with public tax moneys; second, the market effect on hides (religion) of government action with respect of beef (education) is not a subsidy of hides (religion). A different formulation of this "test" of constitutionality is that as long as the society is collectively subsidizing the constitutionally permissible thing—beef or literacy—that should end the inquiry, and the statute should be valid, regardless of any further market effects of that subsidy on other "products." Or, put in terms of the Court's formula for "aid to religion" cases, this approach argues that the *primary effect* of the intervention is that society obtains what it wants (say, more beef or more literacy); the fact that beef and hides (education and religion in parochial schools) are jointly supplied simply produces an unavoidable *side effect*.[9]

With this reasoning West seems to conclude that the Court's recent decision in *Nyquist*,[10] which struck down New York's program to provide tuition reimbursement and income tax credit to users of private scnools, is unwise.[11]

I agree that the Establishment clause should not preclude the state from pursuing secular objectives simply because religious interests and the secular interests are interdependent. Otherwise, the very exercise of private religious beliefs would dominate and circumscribe legitimate and desired nonsectarian, collective action. Therefore, a "test" of constitutionality, in which "market effects" on religion—to use the Westian phrasing—are sufficient to strike down the statute, seems wrong. On the contrary, I think it crucial for the secular aspects of a program to be able to save it from unconstitutionality.

Let me briefly consider three "tests" which have such a focus in order to illustrate the point. (1) Surely it cannot be that legislation with *any* favorable effect on religion is unconstitutional; careful tracing could document some beneficial impact of nearly any program. (2) Nor will it do to limit the principle to laws which the legislature *knew* would benefit religion. Opponents of any bill—regardless of the basis of their opposition—would be sure to employ some of those many social scientists who ask about these days to bring such (potential) beneficial effects to the attention of the legislature. Hence, to take up West's example, a government tree-cutting program would be invalidated if it could be pointed out in advance that by generating sawdust it would, among other things, lower the price of church incense. (3) Even if the principle were limited to cases in which there was (or the legislature knew there would be) a *large* beneficial impact on religion, it would intolerably inhibit secular government action. For example, perhaps building roads and running public transportation on Sunday may be shown to have large beneficial impacts on religion. Notwithstanding this unfortunate aspect of an Establishment clause "test," which strikes down laws solely on the basis of their "market effects" on religion, one view of the Court's recent opinions is that this is precisely its approach. Under this view, while it is not any effect that dooms the law, the Court is nonetheless seen as finding programs unconstitutional because their market effects are rather visible. Indeed, West seems to draw this conclusion from the Court's work. As for what is "visible enough," the damning visibility may seemingly be evidenced by a variety of factors: the religious-based political alignment responsible for the passage of the bill or the religious-based nature of the political fight over the bill, the religious identity of the bill's beneficiaries, the clarity of the connection between the bill and its market effects, or perhaps simply the ease with which those market effects may be imagined. If this is what the Court is doing, society seems stuck with the result that it will be inhibited from efficiently pursuing (or perhaps pursuing at all) collective, secular objectives, whose accomplishment inevitably produces visible ties with religion because of the interdependency of religion with the particular secular objective. Whether a test of "visibility" of this sort produces any worse results than are produced by any other plausible tests is an open question which I leave to the reader to ponder after reading the remainder of the text in this section.

For me the concerns underlying the Establishment clause could be satisfied with an affirmative answer to this hypothetical question: Would the legislature have acted as it did were there no interdependency with religion involved? If so, then I think it would be fair to say that there is no subsidy of religion, that the religious benefits are constitutionally permitted side effects. But since it is not feasible to psychoanalyze the legislators who voted for the law, and because members may be motivated to vote for a bill for a variety of reasons, in order for the courts to exercise judicial review there must be a more objective way of determining whether the "reason" for the legislation was secular—that is, whether its enactment depended upon the favorable religious impact.

And the problem with the Westian constitutional formulation, as I have thus far stated it, is that it is based on the *assumption* that the reason behind the legislative action is increased private production of secular education. But how do we know this to be the case? The legislature, too, will realize that a decision to cast a program in the form of a subsidy of the purchase of one jointly supplied good will have a market impact on the other good.

Therefore, how is one to escape the possibility that the reason for the enactment was precisely to have that impact on religion, and that the legislature is not at all interested in increased private education—that is, it would not pursue this stimulation of private education but for the interdependency of religion? To be sure, this way of aiding religion may be thought clumsy, but the legislature also knows about the First Amendment, and hence realizes that open assistance is clearly unacceptable to the Supreme Court.[b] And, for this same reason it also will not suffice to rely on a legislative declaration that its purposes are secular. We must somehow go behind both the form of the law and what the legislature says about it, yet without going into the minds of its members. What objective indicia we should look for, I think, is the great issue in the "aid to religion" cases.[c]

A number of more or less objective approaches are possible. I will briefly comment on three of them. One involves examining the political position of the program's beneficiaries. For example, in a case like *Nyquist,* it may be argued that since those New Yorkers whose religious exercise is in fact aided by the subsidy are members of religious minorities (mainly Catholics), we can count on the objectives of the political majority (non-Catholics) to be secular. In many respects I find this rather convincing; what troubles me is that it is plausible that, despite the "minority" status of those directly aided, the legislative plan is part of a logrolling trade-off of aid to a minority religion in return for votes on, say, related and controversial issues such as abortion or contraception. Such logrolling might be a very sensible way to maximize individual choice in a world without the First Amendment, but ours is not that world, and thus such trading seems not allowed. And since the Court could not hope to discover accurately whether such logrolling actually occurred (if this is an important fear), such an approach is unsatisfactory. Moreover, it does not provide a helpful solution in places where Catholics are in the majority, or where the effect of the statute is to aid Protestants in the exercise of their religion— unless it is to strike down such statutes despite an interdependent and truly desired secular reason for them. That would be an unfortunate result, I think, unless there were no other way out of the dilemma.

A second approach is to try to compare the benefits of a program to religion with its secular benefits, and to hold the program unconstitutional if the religious benefits dominate. The underlying rationale for this approach would be that when the secular gains are (relatively) slight, it is unlikely that the legislature would have acted were there no religious

[b] Moreover, the form of the aid in most of the decided cases is ambiguous; although the subsidy is said to be for beef (private education), it is clear that most of those who use the subsidy are, in fact, buying the whole cow including the hide (education and religion together).

[c] I do not think this problem is any way solved by the Court's willingness to concede in all these cases that the law "reflects a clearly secular purpose." That reflection does not reveal whether the law would have been enacted without the interdependency of religion.

interdependency. However, it is difficult to know on what terms such a comparison would be made, let alone how a Court could properly make the necessary calculations. One possibility is simply to identify, label, and count the beneficiaries, that is, to determine whether most or only few beneficiaries are directly aided in their religious exercise by the program. This approach may be criticized on a number of grounds, however: (1) The Court will not be able to decide whom to label as the beneficiaries of the program. (2) Clever legislative logrolling will result in packaging programs together in a way which end-runs such an approach in any event. (3) Counting and labeling beneficiaries is an unfair approximation of secular and sectarian benefits, if for no other reason than that beneficiaries aided in their religious exercise may also be aided in their secular pursuits. Moreover, this approach concedes that the pursuit of secular objectives would still be frustrated when there was no good alternative means available which did not involve largely benefiting persons in connection with their religious exercise.

Nonetheless, this count-the-numbers technique may best characterize what the Court is doing, as Chief Justice Burger claimed in his *Nyquist* dissent. In *Nyquist,* the Court plainly saw the beneficiaries of New York's tuition credit plan as those families who use private, largely religious, schools, by providing what the state claimed to be educational fairness to the child beneficiaries and financial equity to their parents. Since this is a group essentially comprised of those assisted in their exercise of religious freedom by the program, the plan would fail under the "numbers" test. Suppose, however, the Court had been made to see the plan differently—as a voluntary redemption of the child's state constitutional right to attend public school for a price to the state far below what it would have cost to provide that education. In that event, the beneficiaries, or certainly most of them, would be taxpayers who are not especially aided in their religious exercise, and the plan would be valid under the "numbers" test. The same result would follow if the Court had been made to see the plan as encompassing the state's whole school finance scheme, for public and private schools alike. But how is the Court to decide how to "see" it? And what about the fact that financially assisted religious school users in either case are directly helped with secular objectives? This example may be enough to convince some that choosing a proper class of beneficiaries to be counted and labeled is a misguided and unprincipled task.[12]

A third approach is to concentrate only on the secular purposes the legislature claims to be advancing and then to make a judgment about whether the "deal" the state claims to have made is bona fide. One way to do that is to ask whether the state is getting its money's worth in secular benefits.[13] For example, under this approach it would be all right for the state to acquire fruitcakes from a monastery if it paid the market price, but it would be unconstitutional to pay an inflated price.

There are two main difficulties with this approach. First, how do we know the state would want fruitcakes at any price were they not made and sold by the monastery? If the product were acquired through competitive bidding, we probably could be confident that the nature of the seller was irrelevant to the government. But in the absence of competitive bids—and there were none in the "aid to religion" cases—we are forced either to assume the state wants fruitcakes or to conclude that as long as the state is obtaining full value in secular products or services for its money, it is no poorer, and then taxpayers simply cannot complain that government resources have been diverted for religious purposes. These both are rather unsatisfactory responses to what I have characterized as the central underlying question: Would the transaction have occurred in the absence of the religious interdependency?

The more serious problem with this approach involves valuing what the state obtains. One cannot say simply that since the state paid, it must have gained what it wanted, for this would empty this test of any content other than unbridled deference to the legislature. This means that the Court will have to decide whether the state obtains value for money, and I assume that will mean an "objective" valuation. But I have serious doubts about the competence of the Court to make such valuation, for it involves deciding terribly difficult empirical questions. Take the *Nyquist* situation, for example. Seemingly the Court would at least have to inquire into how much additional private secular education was provided as a result of the plan and how much that is worth to the state. But how can it determine that? Moreover, is the Court also to determine how many children did not transfer into public schools as a result of the program and how much that is worth?

While Choper realizes that he may be open to attack on the grounds that these empirical issues may be very difficult to determine, he takes refuge in the fact that under his formula there can be little doubt that the society is obtaining its money's worth when the amount of aid given is, as has been true in all the cases thus far litigated, well under half of what is spent on children in the public schools. This is true because he compares the amount paid with the *total* value of the secular education provided by religious schools. The problem I have with this method is that it is not clear why the state aid should be compared with the value of the *total secular education* provided.

Voluntarism is already creating secular benefits for which the collectivity need not pay; if what we are to envision is a process whereby the collectivity is seen to be purchasing secular education through religious schools, its agents would be rather poor negotiators if they agreed to pay for everything previously provided freely—unless that were necessary for any continued private provision at all. It is like paying for fruitcakes when you know the monastery is giving them away and would continue to do so regardless of your payment. This is not a bona fide "deal"; it is income redistribution in favor of religion.

There is yet another difficulty with this test. An objective determination of whether the state obtains value for its money, whether it is in terms of changed family or private school behavior (of an input or outcome sort), may require waiting until quite some time after the legislation has been put into effect, since the payoffs may not be immediately forthcoming. However, the Court presently is willing and accustomed to judge the "aid to religion" cases before the programs start operating—perhaps in part so as to avoid finding itself in the position of fashioning a remedy in the event of past unconstitutional payment of funds in violation of the First Amendment.

The upshot is that each of the three approaches to the Establishment clause which I have discussed has shortcomings; and I am confident that other universal "objective" tests would as well. Thus, perhaps we should not be surprised that the Court's opinions seem to have no consistent principle and that many cases seem irreconcilable or appear to turn on whether the "aid" is thought to be inherently secular, despite West's demonstration of the economic meaninglessness of this notion.

On the other hand, perhaps the Court can do better than this—if not with a single universal test consistently applied, then at least with some general rules as to the types of considerations that are to be allowed in different kinds of cases. One approach would be to adopt rules for certain types of cases while using techniques of the *prima facie* case and shifts in the burden of proof in others. For example, in de jure cases, where the form of the government transfer is religious in nature (such as a distribution of prayerbooks or the building of churches) or where religious exercise is a condition for receiving the transfer (such as a $10 payment to those who attend church), the program might always be struck down and the state barred from arguing that the reason for the plan is the secular benefit generated by it. (Such programs might also violate the Fourteenth Amendment's equal protection clause.) Nor, perhaps, would the result differ if the scope of the distribution were expanded to include secular items; that is, prayerbooks could not be distributed along with readers, nor churches built along with gymnasiums, for their inclusion would be presumed to be intended for the purpose of, and having the effect of, aiding religious exercise. Similarly, when the state acquires secular goods or services through competitive bid, perhaps all such transactions will be upheld and opponents not permitted to argue that the reason for the purchase was the government's wish to benefit religious-group-owned suppliers. So too, when unrestricted cash is distributed to persons on the basis of formal criteria unrelated to religion or religious exercise, such as welfare or social security, perhaps no challenge arising out of alleged religious uses of the money will be entertained. In short, in these cases, at both ends of the spectrum, judicial inquiry into reasons or effects would be minimal.

By contrast, in other cases the Court might be willing to look closely at both reasons and effects with the burden of proof assigned on the basis of *prima facie* characteristics of the program. For example, perhaps in cases in which the bulk of those who receive a government transfer conditioned on some secular behavior (or the bulk of any identified subclass established by a statute) can be shown to be pursuing religious objectives through that behavior, the Court will closely scrutinize the program's effects with the burden falling on the state to demonstrate objectively that the new secular benefits obtained are worth the funds transferred. This should induce the legislature, in cases such as *Nyquist,* to leave a clear and convincing trail as to both reasons and anticipated impacts, if it can. What it would take to convince the Court, of course, is a difficult question. But at least in *Nyquist* the following arguments could be made and would have to be addressed by the state: (1) If the legislature is interested in children's educational equity, and not religious education, why did it not demand higher standards from private schools? (2) Unless it is to assist religious education, why were parents who mainly use religious schools singled out for relief from paying for public schools when single people and the childless were not relieved?

On the other hand, when the bulk of the recipients of a conditioned transfer are evidently not pursuing religious objectives through the conduct required for the benefit, the burden might be put on challengers to prove that nonetheless the state is not obtaining fair value in secular benefits (or perhaps that religious effects outweigh secular effects after which the burden would be shifted back to the state to justify the expenditure by the secular benefits obtained). This kind of rule would be applied, for example, in the case of tax deductions for day-care expenditures where opponents protest the placement of children by some families in church facilities where religious indoctrination accompanies the day-care service.

Actually selecting the appropriate classes of cases for the appropriate per se or *prima facie* case rule would require a nice exercise of judgment, as would fitting ambiguous cases into the proper category. At least, however, there could be established a consistent pattern of judicial review in which twin concerns which seem to go toward uncovering the reason for the enactment—are the beneficiaries using the government aid for religious purposes, and what kind of secular advantage is the state really obtaining?—would both be brought to bear in an intuitively sensible manner. It also avoids forcing the Court to decide in each case for itself what is the value of the secular benefits generated by the legislation under scrutiny.

Predictions and Recommendations

Next I will turn to West's suggestions and observations as to what the citizens of the several states might do now that they have had certain attempts to transfer resources to private schools or their users struck down as violating the Establishment clause. One view of this is that if the objective of the voters or the legislature is to do, in another form, what they have already been forbidden to do, then the Court will find a way, no matter how it is couched, to strike the statute down. That is, the Court will reason from concern for its institutional integrity and will worry less about the doctrinal sensibilities of its new holdings. Its agressive efforts to force racial integration in southern schools in the face of governmental efforts to evade its basic holdings about school segregation may be characterized as an example of this.

West's expressed view is that what will protect his proposals is that their effects with respect to religion will be much less visible than was true in those cases where statutes have been invalidated. He also seems to think that certain changes are in some sense so far removed from religious schools that the Court would not dare reach out and strike them down, even if it realizes their effects. I believe that what is more important is that his proposals have attributes which differ from those of past schemes, and that because there are bona fide, independent objectives served by them, the Court may be convinced that to uphold them does not run counter to its past decisions against "aid to religion."

Today people pay taxes to support public schools in amounts which West believes are out of line with the benefits they receive; this is particularly so for nonusers. Users of nonpublic schools have the added burden—voluntarily undertaken—of paying again. These two points lead to a series of possible "reforms" which I will divide into two classes: (1) those which focus only on changing public school finance, and (2) those which also focus on changing private school finance.

Changes Aimed at the Public School Side

West suggests first that future *increases* in public school costs be financed by user charges or taxes; he rightly notes that this will benefit users of nonpublic schools since they will have more money left to spend on private school tuition than they would have were the increase financed by general school taxes as is the present and anticipated pattern. I agree that this proposal is not likely to be found to violate the Establishment clause. However, it is not simply the low visibility of the effect on private school users that is involved. The shift from general to user taxes also is designed to (and would) have a redistributive impact among persons who are not private school users: first, it would provide tax relief for those who do not and will not have children; second, it would shift the burden from those with few children toward those with many—assuming, as I think West intends, that the user tax or fee be paid per child. West is not insensitive to the poor; once the fees or user taxes become very substantial, the poor would be relieved of further payment.[14]

A second suggestion of his is to the same effect, only more so: public schools would charge users their full costs (not just their increased costs). However, long-term loans (or loan guarantees) would be made available by government to parents of public school users; this would allow parents to finance the education of their chilren over a substantial period, rather than merely during those years in which their children are in school[d]; I assume that poor parents would be allowed to repay the loans on an income-contingent basis. Under this plan, nonpublic school users and those who will go without children are helped even more, since the existing general school taxes would largely be eliminated.[e] The burden on larger public school user families will be especially increased.

In view of our long tradition of "free" public schools, I have some doubts about the current political feasibility of either of these solutions, particularly in view of a third possibility which I now offer: it is simply that voters and legislators turn down requests by school authorities for increased funds. Because of inflation, over time this will diminish the quality of the public school offering, and I presume (perhaps naively) that public schools will begin to contract their programs. Families will then purchase more and more supplemental education in the private market on a full-cost basis. Notice that, unless the poor are given increased welfare, they may be worse off under this approach than under West's proposals; indeed, the fact that the poor might come out the losers is another reason why this third possibility might be more politically feasible than West's two plans. In fact, some might argue that the recent rash of local school bond issue failures and school tax override defeats represent this phenomenon already at work—that the crucial negative votes of private school users and nonusers defeat the measures.[f]

---

[d] The reason that the government loan scheme would be beneficial is that the present private capital market seems unwilling to make long-term loans to families who have no tangible collateral to post. Perhaps the usury, bankruptcy, and slavery laws account for this "market failure."

[e] They would not entirely be eliminated if the plan looked to taxpayers generally, instead of to borrowers, to provide funds needed to cover administrative costs, defaults, and principal waivers for, say, poor families.

[f] Economists Norton Grubb and Jack Osman, through the Childhood and Government Project at the University of California (Berkeley) are currently studying the relationship of local public school spending to non-user characteristics of the district.

What troubles me about these various "reforms" is that they are advanced with too little concern about how they may alter what may be argued to be current commitments to child equity. And while "proper" child equity policy is a normative question, it is one about which people have feelings and upon which people base their votes and their actions. For example, are the relatively altered positions of large and small families (hurting the former) which all these plans would produce "fair"? At present the public education a child receives—at least the funds spent on her/him—is not dependent upon the number of siblings she or he has, although probably the amount of goods and services provided to the child by her/his parents is.[15] Charging families for public school cost increases on a per-child basis will particularly decrease the well-being of larger families which use public schools, and the burden of that decrease might be shouldered by the child members of such families. If so, while their education will not depend upon family size because the family will pay the school tax, their other development will; e.g., money used for schooling will be unavailable for toys or shoes. Under full-cost public schooling, even with government loan schemes, larger families might well be induced to shift to less desired, lower-cost private schools to reduce their long-term financial burden. If so, then family size and educational spending will become interdependent.

The desirability of this must be confronted. Perhaps this result will induce families to have fewer children—only as many as they can "afford" without family size educational subsidies—and some would find this desirable on a number of grounds. Indeed, some would consider it long overdue. But the condition of children who are, in fact, born into large families, which under current conditions would use public schools, may be significantly worsened; that, it seems to me, represents a change in policy which should not be forgotten in the rush to aid families using nonpublic schools. Of course, this impact might be largely remedied by charging families one fee or tax regardless of the number of school users in the family; and other in-between alternatives are also imaginable.

The main point, I think, is that any plan which "benefits" users of nonpublic schools must be paid for. Thus we must be carefully attentive to whether the burden of that payment falls on those we think appropriate to bear it, and we must think about those who pay not only in terms of the income of adults but also in terms of family size.

My sense is that, apart from education, in America today we are ambivalent about how the financial burden faced by large families should be carried. We are very reluctant to take any *direct* action either to limit the right of parents to bear children or to force them to exercise that right; and in turn we tend to feel that if they have many children, the entire brood is both theirs to keep and their responsibility. Yet because of our concern for the children born, we are, at the same time, unhappy about large poor families but reluctant to allow the children to be forced to depend only on their parents and private charity. Thus, we act indirectly and perhaps inconsistently; for example, we provide a welfare mother with both birth control counseling and extra funds for each additional child she has.[16]

Changes Also Aimed at the Private School Side

In addition to benefiting users of nonpublic schools by relieving them from existing and/or future public school tax burdens, it may be possible to benefit them in other ways as well without running afoul of the Establishment clause.

West's suggestions rely on various ways of treating equally families who use both types of schools. At least three possibilities are worth noting. (1) If public schools are priced at full cost, then government loans (or guarantees) may be made available not only to public school user families, but to private school users as well. (2) Education vouchers—in amounts somewhere in the ballpark of the amount currently spent per child in public schools—may be made available to all families and used as payment of (or toward) tuition at the public or private school of the family's choice. (3) Or the government may pay for outcomes, not inputs—that is, not to send a child to school but for the child's educational attainment.

Loans and Vouchers. West argues that the Court will probably agree that government loans available to all do not violate the Establishment clause on the grounds that this financial assistance is obviously secular and sufficiently removed from religion so as to be treated like reimbursement for bus rides to private schools; he is concerned, however, that the Court would not approve the voucher scheme. I disagree, based upon my estimation of what family responses would be under *either* plan. I predict that in both cases many more families than do so today would leave the public schools and would purchase private nonreligious education for their children. In a climate in which the dominant theme is that children attend any school which their families prefer, rather than public schools to which they are assigned by professionals, chosen attendance at religious schools will play a subordinate role. In short, recreating the role of families in education, including their right to employ religious schools, is not a program adopted and maintained because some are able to choose religious education. In such event, I believe that whatever test the Court employs, it may be convinced to uphold both voucher and loan schemes.

Choosing between the two proposals on their merits raises difficult policy questions which override church-state issues. First, there is the family size issue discussed above. But note that both plans could be squeezed to fit either resolution of that question; that is, the voucher could be awarded on a per-family rather than per-child basis, and the loan repayment obligation could be, say, waived for users beyond the first child in the family.

Second, and more important, the voucher approach indirectly coerces family "spending" on education to a greater extent than does the loan scheme. Under the latter, to the extent that a family elected to use its money not for education, but for, say, the child's health or for the parents' pleasure (e.g., whiskey), the burden of the society's education program borne by such a family would be limited.

By contrast, under the voucher plan, the family would be taxed substantially in any case, thereby leaving it with less disposable income; and since it would also forfeit large economic benefits if it were to refuse the voucher it would probably be induced to spend at least that much.[g] Of course, many children would, in fact, have as much money spent on their education under either plan; but surely this would not invariably be true. Still, it is unclear whether either the children or the society will be better or worse off as a result of the differing spending patterns. It would depend upon how much is gained from extra educational spending as compared with the spending of extra unrestricted family income. Many will fear that when there is less indirect coercion toward spending for education, some children will be severly shortchanged, to the detriment of both the children and society; in addition, I suspect that many who think this way will also believe it unwieldy to protect such children and society through the neglect laws. Hence, they would probably prefer the voucher to the loan scheme out of pragmatism, if not principle.

Finally, unless the loan repayments were income-contingent, the voucher plan would probably be more beneficial to the poor than an education loan plan.[17] But is this the proper comparison? I expect that, looking at the big picture, West would argue for a combined educational loan scheme (not income-contingent) and income transfer program instead of an educational voucher plan, and in many ways this is quite appealing. Imagine the San Francisco welfare mother with three children who receives today, say, $4,500 a year of cash public assistance, food, stamp bonuses, and medical care, and whose children each have about $2,000 per year spent on them by the San Francisco public schools. If that $2,000 each, or $6,000 total, could be turned into cash for the family instead given in educational vouchers, in many cases the whole family might well be better off. As a matter of current political reality, however, I believe that persons

[g]Compulsory education laws requiring a minimum amount of spending on a child's schooling, either directly or implicitly, could reduce the potential expenditure differences between the loan and voucher schemes.

willing to vote for redistributions to the poor are far more willing to approve something they think the poor should have than to approve transfers of unrestricted cash above that amount needed to satisfy minimum food, shelter, and medical needs.

Paying for Results. Paying families for the educational accomplishments of their children (for example, by being able to pass high school graduate equivalency exams) in order to induce provision of efficient education by parents is a very intriguing suggestion. It presumes that the private incentives, such as jobs with higher pay or status, are insufficient to induce the amount of educational attainment that children deserve or that society wants. At the same it argues that unsuccessful educational efforts help neither children nor society, and should not be collectively supported. I concur that such a plan should not run afoul of the Establishment clause, but once again I have some serious problems with the proposal itself.

First, I am troubled about the ability of poorer families to finance the inputs necessary to generate the educational attainment that would be eventually rewarded. This would probably necessitate loan schemes. For those who borrowed, while the plan might be very effective, I would be concerned about the psychological pressures generated within the family when a large portion of the parents' *future* income depends upon the child's educational attainment.

Second, unless the attainments which triggered the bonus payment were individualized, some would earn it easily, some would do so with great sacrifice, and some simply could not earn it at all. This means both that the incentives are not very finely tuned and that the equitable right to payment is questionable. Moreover, it is likely that the poor would have to make greater financial outlays than would the rich in order to bring their children up to the minimum attainment needed to earn the bonus. In the best of payment-for-results worlds, society would probably wish to pay only to induce results that otherwise would not be attained; yet, to estimate how well a child would have done without the bonus payment and to compare that attainment with how well he or she has done in order to determine the appropriate payment raises staggering measurement problems in view of the present state of the art.

Nonetheless, while subject to some of the same objections, a somewhat modified version of this scheme might well be a suitable basis for experimentation (at least for children not clearly suffering from mental retardation): When the child reaches age 5, all families would be given an educational voucher to be used at the public or private kindergarten of their choice. If at age 6 the child demonstrated the necessary first grade or reading readiness desired by the state, the family would be awarded an educational voucher for the next year, again to be used at the public or private school desired, and so on. That is, as long as the child could demonstrate each year grade level competence in the learning areas required by the state, his/her education would remain under the direction of the parents and financed with the voucher. If the child failed to meet the state requirements, then the parents would be required to send the child to schools run by the state, at least until such time as the child "caught up." Concerns that the state would demand too much should be mitigated, I think, by the fact that the public schools voluntarily chosen would, in effect, be held to the same standards. Concerns that the state would require the "wrong things" are more troubling. But one point of the experiment is to try to force the society to spell out just what it does want from schooling.

Conclusion

One of the most helpful aspects of West's contribution is that by suggesting new ways of thinking about state aid to users of private (including religious) schools, he stimulates us to rethink entirely our reasons for funding public education as we now do. If a thorough reexamination of this matter by our society is the result of the *Nyquist* case, it will be a healthy result, regardless of the merits of that particular decision.

Notes

1. In West's *Education and the State* Institute of Economic Affairs, London, (1970 ed.) as well as his other writings, he favors positive pricing of education.

2. *Everson v. Board of Education,* 330 U.S. 1 (1947)—reimbursement of bus transportation costs to parents sending children to private schools.

3. *Board of Education v. Allen,* 392 U.S. 236 (1968)—loaning of textbooks to children attending private schools.

4. *Walz v. Tax Commission,* 397 U.S. 664 (1970)—property tax exemption for charitable organizations, including religious organizations.

5. No Supreme Court case actually holds that general municipal services may be furnished to religious schools, but the Court has often indicated that this is clearly allowed. Indeed, it appears permissible to provide such services to racially discriminating schools even though loaning textbooks to students at such schools is not. See *Norwood v. Harrison,* 413 U.S. 455 (1973).

6. *Committee for Public and Religious Liberty v. Nyquist,* 413 U.S. 756 (1973)—funds earmarked for private school custodial functions. Also

see *Levitt v. Committee for Public Education and Religious Liberty,* 413 U.S. 472 (1973)—funds earmarked for testing.

7. *Nyquist,* see note 6—tuition reimbursement and income tax credit for users of private schools; and *Sloan v. Lemon,* 413 U.S. 825 (1973)—tuition reimbursement for users of private schools.

8. For a discussion of this idea, see Choper, "The Establishment Clause and Aid to Parochial Schools," 56 *Calif. L. Rev.* 260, 319 (1968).

9. The Court's view is that these "aid to religion" cases are to be judged by a three-pronged test. The law "must reflect a clearly secular purpose, . . .must have a primary effect that neither advances nor inhibits religion, . . .[and] must avoid excessive government entanglement with religion." *Nyquist,* see note 6 at 773. In practice the Court does not admit that it is inquiring into purpose other than to note that the legislature has taken the trouble to declare a secular purpose. The key to what the Court is doing lies in what it calls the law's "primary effect," and it is to this issue that West's joint supply model is centrally directed.

10. *See* note 6.

11. So, too, I take it, is the Court's decision in *Lemon v. Kurtzman,* 403 U.S. 602 (1971)—state payment of 15 percent of the salary of private school teachers of secular subjects. The Court invalidated that plan on "entanglement grounds:" that the state would too much interfere with religion in applying its administrative safeguards to assure the funds were used for secular purposes. But if religious schools are concerned about entanglement with the state through the state's administrative supervision, they can elect not to participate in the program; and the Court should not be concerned on their behalf. Otherwise the Court is in the awkward position of precluding from access to a program those who think it will help them, essentially on the grounds that it will hurt *them.*

12. For further evidence that the group the Court "sees" as the beneficiaries of the program is important to the outcome, see *Sloan v. Lemon,* 413 U.S. 832 (1973), where Justice Powell, in striking down Pennsylvania's private school tuition reimbursement program, states that the "State has singled out a class of its citizens for a special economic benefit"—meaning users of private, mainly religious, schools. See also the recent decision in *Meek v. Pittinger,* 95 S. Ct. 1753 (1975), where the Court upheld Pennsylvania's textbook loan program but invalidated its program of loaning instructional material and equipment. The Court saw "all schoolchildren"—public and private school users alike—as the beneficiaries of the textbook loans, whereas it saw the "primary beneficiaries . . .[of the] instructional material and equipment loan provisions . . .[as] nonpublic schools wirh a predominant sectarian character" [at 1761 and 1763]. Why the beneficiaries of the materials and equipment program

weren't all schools or all schoolchildren is not explained, even though materials and equipment are plainly made available to and in public schools as well. The Court does distinguish the book program on the grounds that the books were loaned to the children; but, of course, the fact that the tax credit and tuition reimbursement was made to the parents and not to the school in both *Nyquist* and *Sloan* was held irrelevant. Note finally that *Walz*, note 4, where property tax exemptions for religious organizations were upheld, may also be seen to fit the "numbers" analysis. There the Court clearly saw the beneficiaries as all those charitable groups entitled to the tax benefit, of which religious organizations were seen to be a nondominant portion. It is fair to note, however, that the Court also distinguished *Walz* on the grounds that the exemption was very long standing and that the exemption helped free the state from entanglement with religious groups.

13. My description of this approach is a generalized version, with some modification of my own, of that recommended by Choper. His test is this: "Govermental financial aid may be extended directly or indirectly to support parochial schools without violation of the establishment clause so long as such aid does not exceed the value of the secular educational service rendered by the school." 56 *Calif. L. Rev.* at 465-66.

14. Because of this treatment of the poor, the proposal is not likely to violate the equal protection clause. See *San Antonio Independent School District v. Rodriguez,* 411 U.S. 1, n. 60 (1973), where the Court intimated that depriving children of public education entirely, because their families could not afford the fees, might be unconstitutional. Notice, however, that West would charge poor user families, through fees or charges, amounts equal to those general taxes from which they would be relieved. Charging parents for schooling their children, whether called tuition or a user tax, might violate many state constitutions which require "free" public schools. These provisions have recently been litigated in a number of cases challenging school textbook fees.

15. Economists Norton Grubb and David Stern, through the Childhood and Government Project at the University of California (Berkeley), are currently studying intrafamilial spending patterns. We presently know too little about this.

16. Some states impose a ceiling on the family's welfare grant, regardless of the number of added children. This has been upheld as constitutional in *Dandridge v. Williams*, 397 U.S. 471 (1970).

17. Of course, the advantage of the voucher plan could be blunted were it financed by a highly regressive tax. If the loan repayments are made income-contingent, then the loan plan looks like a voucher plan in which (1) the voucher must be purchased for a price that is based on family income, and (2) the value of the voucher—at least up to the maximum loan

available—may be determined by the family. In this form the scheme is remarkably similar to the "family power equalizing" plan which Coons, Clune, and I have proposed in *Private Wealth and Public Education*, Harvard, Cambridge, (1970), pages 256-268.

Response to Sugarman: Public Economics and the Free Exercise Clause

E.G. West

On the main issues that I raise in my essay Sugarman seems to have gone right to the heart of matters and joined the debate in a welcome and constructive way. It is symbolic of his grasp of the issues I was trying to grapple with that in the title to his essay he places quotation marks around the word "aid." This focuses straight away on the question of whether channeling education tax funds from poor people (and others) through the political process and back to the same people in the form of public education *can* be described as *aid*. My proposal short-circuited this system by making further increments of taxes necessary to pay for increased costs, going this time *directly* from the taxpayer to the point of supply—the school. It is reassuring that Sugarman endorses this proposal with a legal, professional, opinion when he observes, "I agree that this proposal is not likely to be found to violate the Establishment clause." Strictly this is really all that is relevant to the *main* argument of my essay. That argument was couched in terms of positive economics. It set out to find a solution to the problem of finding a method that would satisfy all major parties in the Nyquist "dispute," and especially the Supreme Court.

Like his colleague Coons, Sugarman nevertheless expresses some lurking concern about the possible redistributive effect of the proposal. I submit once more that these considerations are peripheral to my inquiry in the terms in which I set it up. The question there concerned the prediction of the likelihood of successful adoption of a system that respects the wishes of the political members of the government, the middle voters, and the members of the Supreme Court—and almost regardless of the niceties of redistribution effects at the lower end of the income scale. This is not to say that I am not personally concerned about these effects—only that these relate to an alternative, normative investigation and not to the particular exercise in positive economics that I was concerned with.

Again I am not unwilling to enter into the field of value judgments, provided this does not detract from my main endeavor as above, and provided that readers keep the normative, positive distinction clearly before them. I appreciate Sugarman's describing me as being "not insensitive to the poor." This rules out the tiresome game of who can score most in intensity of outrage on behalf of the poor. He has also well received my initial signals on this matter when he describes me as being prepared to allow transfers, where necessary, to the poorest.

On other matters I can only repeat briefly some of the points made in reply to Coons. First, my own historical researches convince me that the degree of "irresponsibility" alleged to belong to families prior to state intervention has been much exaggerated. Second, if, on grounds of "child equity," the parental irresponsibility problem needs important attention, the laws on compulsion are an important avenue for securing it. Third, the problem of financial inability has to be seen in terms of the family's *lifetime* tax contribution and lifetime income. I suspect that Sugarman may have overlooked the latter point to some extent in expressing his concern that a shift to user taxes would provide tax relief for those who do not have children. Young adults who are not married and have no children certainly escape the user tax at the present moment; but this does not mean they will escape it during their lifetime, because there is a high probability that they will have children in the future. Sugarman raises a nice point when he refers to those families who have above-average numbers of children and asks whether a user tax that is equivalent to the taxes that this family now pays will be a detrimental change to poor families in these circumstances. Before answering this question precisely, one must know how "well off" such families are under the present system. I quoted figures (in Tables 1 and 2, pages 13 and 25) showing the tax contributions of families within different income groups. These figures were not broken down to more exact measurements of the variance in tax contribution according to family size. We must remember, therefore, that positive variance does exist. The family with the larger number of children normally pays more than another family in the same income group in property taxes (or its equivalent in the form of rent incidence), sales taxes, and other indirect taxes. In the strictest version of my proposal the families with the largest number of children would accordingly receive *greater* conventional tax relief and would therefore be able to afford larger user tax total expenditures. Beyond this then there can, if necessary, be special transfers on behalf of this section of society. I see no reason for refusing to switch generally to a user tax system for 90 or 95 percent of the populace because the other 5 or 10 percent *might* be injured, when it is possible to ensure against their injury by alternative means.

I must next reemphasize that the most serious inequity within the present system is the lack of choice. Insofar as the switch to a user tax system promotes this choice, such inequity begins to be undermined and a more efficient system responding to the consumer needs will gradually establish itself. This will begin to provide absolute benefits for the poor, benefits that the rich already enjoy. A given dollar of expenditure, in other words, may provide more education than previously for the very poorest (those with families of large numbers of children) after user tax method has been adopted. It has been reported that the per-pupil cost ratio is 2-to-5 between public school and catholic school pupils.[1] Can anyone doubt that a considerable part of the difference consists of very heavy and excessive administrative overheads in the public system, overheads that the poor would stand, to some extent, to avoid in a more competitive system?

Sugarman's main concern about equity relates to my more tentative long-term proposal where the user tax bears the main burden of financing public school education. My initial plan in the search for a solution to the Nyquist problem was for marginal user taxes to give the same modest tax relief to the parochial schools that was attempted by the New York government. I agree that there are more points to discuss concerning the longer-term possibility of a more "ambitious" reliance on user taxes. This was the reason that I introduced a loan system, a system which Sugarman accepts in principle. He asks the important question of whether poor parents would be allowed to repay the loans on an *income-contingent* basis. I am glad that he raised this question, for it again takes us back to first principles.

Consider once again the fundamental question of why the state intervenes in education in the first place. Imagine initially that there is no financial problem and that families are purchasing education just as they purchase food and clothes for their children. Some would argue that even here there is a case for intervention in order to achieve what is called "social mixing," "integration," or some similar goal. In the present case, such an objective seems to be ruled out because both the *Nyquist* court and New York State argued for what they called more "pluralism." (The temper of the times seems to be to consider that the "melting pot" function of the American public school has been overdone.) The next conventional justification for intervention is on the lines of the external benefits that I outlined. Several writers in this book are uncomfortable with this concept, and I share much of their skepticism. (My fullest response to it is contained in my replies to Milton Friedman and Murray Rothbard.) At most, it is likely that "externalities" can explain only a fraction of the amount of intervention. In any case, when marginal externalities are alleged to be positive, this is often asserted on the grounds that the average parent cannot *afford* to purchase beyond a certain amount of education for her/his children. "Society" should therefore finance marginal expansion beyond this family optimum level because externalities exist at this particular margin. Such an argument assumes that families are purchasing from their *current* incomes rather than their *lifetime* incomes. Other writers are more explicit and point to the basic problem—that it is difficult for a family to draw upon its lifetime income since the capital market is imperfect. This impediment seems to be the main root of all arguments for intervention in current economic literature.

If government can offset a capital market imperfection (this being an extra assumption that often accompanies the whole argument), it is important to probe the nature of the original imperfection. Many writers stress that educational capital is not available in terms comparable to physical capital, because with conventional loans (like house mortgages) the physical asset can be repossessed in case of default. To some extent this kind of reasoning could be semantic. Repossession cannot occur because the law does not allow investors to hold equity stakes in other human beings. Such argument does not constitute a direct proof that the capital market is "imperfect." Markets work only with a given legal framework. Here the framework is "restricted." This is so because the property rights of the worker (to pledge future income against a loan) are curtailed.

It is interesting, however, to probe deeper and ask why it was first necessary to constrain the law and restrict capital markets. A market "blockage" may have been established deliberately by law, and this because of previous inadequacies in markets in the following sense: Almost certainly there was previously no complete set of risk markets that included a market for income-contingent lending accessible to even those individuals from the lowest income groups. The hindrance to the establishment of such a market is likely to have been severe information and policing costs. Because of these "inadequacies" some individuals will be tempted to borrow on a noncontingent basis. This could, in some cases, have results that are socially repugnant. Allowing others to have an equity stake in oneself on a *noncontingent basis* could lead to forms of slavery. To prevent such consequences, governments would be prompted to protect individuals with usury laws and bankruptcy laws; they might deliberately establish the market blockages previously mentioned. *But they should, if it is feasible, also follow up with a government income-contingent loan scheme.*

It is interesting that no government has yet adopted an income-contingent loan scheme in higher education. Governments seem merely to be attempting in their loan schemes to provide arrangements which use the private banking system as distributors and collectors while the federal government acts as guarantor. The incentives of the banks to police and collect government-guaranteed loans in higher education are reduced to a minimum because of the existence of the federal guarantee. Consequently defaults on student debt are high and increasing. Of the $31 million increase asked for in the 1974 American budget, $26 million was targeted for defaults. American defaults on public educational loans increased from 4.5 percent in 1972 to 7.2 percent in 1974. The present public loan systems are not income-contingent systems; if they were, the need to police them would be even more pressing. All this raises the question of whether in higher education present governments are exploiting their comparative advantages in the capital market area, and it can be strongly argued that they are not. Governments have already invested large resources in establishing machinery for tax assessment and collection. The marginal costs of using this machinery for collection of educational loans should be relatively small. With income-contingent loans there is an added advantage. Such loans depend upon the supply of accurate income statements long after the education has been completed. Governments have this knowledge automatically and cheaply through tax statements. Government-sponsored loans therefore have the potential of improving on the private market and thus carrying reduced rates of interest, not because of subsidies supplied from nonusers, but because of those from "genuine" cost reductions in lending. So far, for some unknown or unstated reasons, in the realm of higher education governments have not exploited this obvious comparative-cost advantage: the use of the income tax machinery. In the system of loans that I am proposing, the income tax machinery would be used. The proposal does not replicate strictly but simulates a *loan* system. The tax authorities would use in their traditional role of *tax* (not debt) collectors; and a service will be rendered, as usual, exclusively to the government. Education would be no longer free but at positive cost. Individual families would be able to draw negative income tax in order to enable them to finance such education. Educational institutions could be obliged to notify social security and income tax authorities concerning the details of their clientele, and the families would also be obliged to file a return to the same authorities independently. In this way family obligations would be automatically computerized to provide a check for future tax purposes.

The main virtue of this system is that it reduces considerably the incentive to default. This is because the penalties for false information on income tax are much more serious and predictable than those imposed by separate guaranteed educational loan organizations. The disincentive is more pronounced where the individual automatically forgoes his rights to social security benefits when he defaults on tax. Another reason why defaults will be considerably lower than under a conventional loan system is that a tax, unlike a loan, is not dischargeable through bankruptcy proceedings.

We come now to a recapitulation of the income contingency principle which is at the heart of Sugarman's question. This principle meets the efficiency requirement of providing insurance elements for borrowers who face some uncertainty as to their future income. It also meets the concern of whether it is wise or desirable for the people from low-income origins to take out large amounts of debt. With the income contingency system of loans there is no burden of debt *that must be paid*; repayment falls only on those who earn more than a certain income and can therefore "afford" it. The education tax as a"loan" repayment is to run for a given number of years; the repayment period should allow sufficient time to repay the total borrowing plus market rates of interest.

The amount of redistribution that is involved in such a "loan" system depends, of course, on the length of time over which payments are to be made. At one extreme, at given rates of interest and over long enough repayment times it is possible for everybody to repay from lifetime income. With shorter repayment periods and higher rates of interest some ex post facto redistribution will occur between participants. This redistribution can be seen to a large extent as an insurance element from an *ex ante* standpoint. If all individuals start off with similar chances of success over a lifetime and the future sizes of their families are a stochastic variable, and assuming risk aversion, then it is in everybody's interests to participate in a scheme wherein there will be future marginal compensation by the extra-successful to those who enjoy below-average success. If we measure income as that enjoyed by the average member of each family, then the larger the family, the lower the expected income. The income-contingent loan system would therefore automatically provide relief to those individuals who had an above-average number of children. This would presumably meet Sugarman's requirement. Insofar as individuals do not start out with equal chances because some have more "natural ability" or greater endowments than others, the latter would not voluntarily join such a scheme unless adequate "opt-out" rates were incorporated. Insofar as all persons are compelled to belong to the scheme and to face uniform rates, there will be elements of "coercive" redistribution of the kind, for instance, that is contained in progressive income tax schemes.

All this adds up to a set of tools that will allow us to at least match the redistribution on behalf of large families that exists in the present system. I believe this helps dissolve Sugarman's concern whether such machinery could accompany my proposal. What, however, of his interesting "soliloquy" about the optimum degree of protection of large families? He asks whether society is not inconsistent or ambivalent here. While we tend to feel that if parents have many children, "the entire brood is both theirs to keep and their responsibility," concern for the children once born still leads us to be reluctant to allow them to be forced to depend only on their parents and private charity. The bold raising of such questions is a rare occurrence these days. It reminds me of the debate on this same issue that took place in the 1870s in England. The argument for free schools was urged by the Birmingham League through its spokesman Sir Charles Dilke. He was challenged by Millicent Fawcet that if one was to provide free education, then one should provide free clothes and free food on the same reasoning. The remission of school fees, Fawcet insisted, would have a pauperizing effect; it should be avoided wherever possible because it amounted to a system of outdoor relief. Clearly a Malthusian in days when there was a strong fear of overpopulation, she went all the way with the stark proposal that the stigma of pauperization "ought" to attach to those favored parents who were given the privilege of free remission. It is interesting that Dilke did not reply to Fawcet that free education was justified by concern for the children once born (the reason that Sugarman gives), but simply that there were external benefits from having an educated populace and that these external benefits expressed themselves mainly in the stronger military potential of the country! Equally curiously, Fawcet did not probe the proposed finance of free education to ask the more important question of whether it was to be *really* free. In the nineteenth century indirect taxes accounted for the bulk of government revenues, and the progressive income tax did not exist. Similarly today I consider it important first to ascertain the amount of payment already being undertaken by large families for the education of their children via indirect taxes.

I am pleased that Sugarman agrees that the government loan scheme that accompanies my *long-term* plan does not violate the Establishment clause since such assistance is obviously secular. It can be treated as the provision of *finance* rather than of education; that is, it can be treated just like reimbursement for bus rides to private schools, etc. While agreeing on the loan scheme, however, Sugarman believes that vouchers might have competitive attractions. Selections from these two proposals should be made on their merits on policy issues that override church-state questions. One of these questions is the family-size issue discussed above. I have now explained that my own system can take care of this question. (Another answer is offered by J.M. Buchanan, below.) Sugarman agrees also that whereas the voucher scheme has the advantage that the voucher could be awarded per-family instead of per-child, the loan scheme could match this advantage because the loan repayment obligation could be, for instance, waived for users beyond, say, the second child in the family. A more important advantage of the voucher, he believes, is its coercive feature of compelling a family to spend more on education than the loan scheme would. There seems to be some misunderstanding here. Sugarman interprets my loan scheme as enabling a family to use its money not for education but for the parents' pleasure (e.g., whiskey). In fact the loan scheme would be confined to purchasers of education exclusively. Questions of optimum expenditure level can be resolved through adjustments to the laws on compulsory education and the manner in which they are policed. As an economist, however, I must confess that I am hesitant to jump into measures that prescribe a given quantity of money to be spent on education; my prior concern is that we now get the maximum amount of education for each dollar spent. In other words, laws on compulsion should concentrate on ascertaining that children get a minimum of education, not that they spend a minimum sum upon it; the two may not amount to the same thing—especially when the market is being "loosened up" and competition is beginning to reassert itself. It is worth noting, too, that Sugarman and

Coons, in their support for "family power equalizing" schemes, insist that the family should be allowed the responsibility for determining the amount to which they should "tax" themselves for education.

While I am sympathetic with advocates of the conventional voucher system, I see it as the second best solution. More important, in the present context I believe its chances of surviving judicial scrutiny are very low. As I explain in my essay, it seems clear that the Court would regard vouchers as *aid* from the state. It would thus undermine the whole rationale of my approach. That approach was constantly to emphasize and make as conspicuous as possible the fact that most families are paying for the education of their children, a fact that seems to be recognized by most writers, including several in this book, when they use quotation marks around the word "free" in "free" education. A loan system, even in the unconventional form of my proposal, a form that uses income tax authorities to implement it, does emphasize that the money being spent comes from the lifetime income streams of the spenders and is not an arbitrary intervention and provision by the state from its "public funds." The "negative income tax" amounts handed out by the IRS to enable young families to purchase education can certainly *parallel* Sugarman's vouchers. If we are agreed on the end result that we seek, it is surely better to adopt that form which does not face the uncertainty of a costly ultimate rejection by the Supreme Court.

Such are the main issues that arise from the Sugarman paper. It will be seen there is much common ground between us. The rest of this response will be concerned with one or two incidental matters. In his section entitled "Paying for Results," he rightly observes that the allocation of government prizes for educational accomplishments is a system that presumes that private incentives (such as jobs with higher pay) are insufficient to induce the amount of educational attainment that society wants. In my terms such a system is required only when marginal externalities are positive. Such a system will be rather marginal to the main proposals in my essay. In any case, I express doubts therein of whether marginal externalities are likely to be substantial, and others in this book share the same skepticism. If families enjoy the return of their tax moneys for education and are allowed to spend them directly, then the private demand curve for education (curve D_j in Figure 1) will shift so much to the right that the community demand curve for external benefits may well become irrelevant. All this means that if extra government prizes are to be awarded, then they are likely to be of small magnitude at best. This would seem to answer Sugarman's fear about the psychological pressures generated within the family "when a large proportion of the parent's *future* income depends on the child's educational attainment." The point is that it is not likely to be a *large* proportion of the parents income that is involved.

Now let's turn to his concern that some individuals would earn the government prize more easily than others and to the difficulty of estimating how well a child would have done without the bonus payment. All these problems attach to the *present* system, if that system is rationalized to some extent on grounds of external benefits. I agree with Sugarman that the point of a government prize experiment is to try to force society to spell out just what it does want from schools.

In one point of his argument Sugarman, while agreeing with my proposals in principle, expresses some doubt on the current political feasibility of them in view of the long tradition of "free" public schools. On this matter I can only refer the reader to my reply to Freeman, who made the same point. A tradition of "free" public schools is a tradition of disguise, obscurantism, and ambiguity, as is indicated by the need to use quotation marks around the word "free." I would have thought that the American tradition of candor would have superseded it, especially in these days of increased political sophistication among the general public.

Sugarman offers an alternative proposal which will reach the same ends as those that I aim at. His is the proposal by which voters and legislators turn down requests for increased educational funds. This, together with inflation, will eventually diminish the quality of public school offerings so that programs will be contracted and families will purchase more supplemental education in the private market. My proposal is offered on the assumption that these things are already happening. Indeed it was a politically sponsored initiative that led to the New York State attempts to rescue the parochial schools. My short-term and main proposal would cost the government authorities and taxpayers no more than they already expressed a willingness to pay.

I agree that there were technical mistakes by the state plan's draft as in the *Nyquist* situation—but perhaps for a slightly different reason. Their arguments for child equity and parental equity certainly might have suggested benefits to a limited group, namely those using parochial schools. The drafter's emphasis should have been upon the fact that the benefits accrued to *all* families using education; those using public schools would benefit by the withdrawal of the threat of a decline in their educational standards as parochial school "refugees" crowded their classrooms. But while this would have made a better case, I am still skeptical that it could have passed the Court.

Sugarman discusses at length the need for the Court to be sure that the reason behind legislative action is increased private production of secular education. He argues that a legislature that wanted to encourage religion could probably do so if it cast its program in the form of subsidies to goods that are jointly supplied with religion. "We must somehow go behind both the form of the law and what the legislature says about it, without going into the minds of its members." In the case of *Nyquist* he feels convinced that there was an objective test of secular intent in the fact that those who received the subsidy were members of religious minorities. Yet he is troubled by the possibility that the legislative plan might have been part of a logrolling trade-off of aid to a minority religion in return for votes on other things. With the First Amendment such trading seems to be precluded. This is certainly an interesting point. But suppose that the legislation *was* in fact the outcome of logrolling. Individuals and groups in society have two main forms of purchasing power: the first is conventional money and the second is "political money." It is no secret that the votes of substantial minorities are valuable to them because of the very existence of logrolling possibilities. To follow up the argument on my proposal, the more that the user tax, or conventional money is used, the less need there is for minorities to use "political money." Again it is a matter of trying to push educational provision away from the conventional modes of the political process. The more this is done, the more Sugarman's problem is solved.

Finally I would like to address to him a question couched in his own terms. If a Supreme Court has the duty to monitor legislation for religious intent, should not the same Court be equally vigilant for the Free Exercise clause as well as the Establishment clause? Historically, should not the Court have intervened when introducing legislation that obliged parochial school users to pay twice for their education? At the moment when a majority begins to cash its substantial "political money" in a fashion that taxes religious minorities in a discriminatory way, would there not have been an obligation on the Court to have arrested the process? The drift of my approach has been to throw more and more focus on the Free Exercise clause, and I have done this via the mechanism of user tax finance for schooling. The public service of parking facilities paid for with parking meter charges is such a user tax system. Charging religious minorities double fees at such meters would surely infringe on the Free Exercise clause. The First Amendment is surely there to protect religions as much as to keep them at arms' length from government's activities. I am a little disappointed that the lawyers have chosen to be silent on this point.

Note

1. This cost ratio is reported in Daniel D. McGarry, "Can Catholic Schools Survive?" *Educational Freedom*, 9 (1): Winter 1970-1971.

Are Externalities Relevant?

Milton Friedman

Over the years, I have become increasingly persuaded that the case for (1) compulsory schooling and (2) government financing of schooling based on supposed externalities is seriously flawed. The flaw is present in my own treatment of these issues in *Capitalism and Freedom* and in West's treatment here.

The flaw is the failure to distinguish between *marginal* and *average* externalities. Suppose private self-interest alone would induce parents to provide schooling to 99.7 percent of all children going through elementary school, to 90 percent through high school, and to 50 percent through college. Let me grant that I, as a representative citizen, would be better off than if the fraction schooled at each level were markedly smaller, say because there is less crime. In this sense, there is an *average* externality; I have benefited from other people's behavior though, by assumption, I have paid none of the costs. But is it obvious that my benefit would be increased if an additional child were schooled at each level? Is it obvious that this would reduce crime further? Indeed, might it not increase it? Are there not negative as well as positive externalities? (Consider the problem of "over-education" in India, for example.) Or more precisely, does not the *net* (positive or negative) externality from extra schooling depend on the amount to which that schooling is added?

To put the matter more concretely, I have never found any plausible argument for net positive externalities from schooling that would not be satisfied if 90 percent, to take an arbitrary figure, received elementary schooling—the three R's. I have yet to see a plausible argument for any net positive marginal externality from additional schooling. But if this be so, and if private interest alone could lead to at least this much schooling—as I believe it is overwhelmingly plausible that it would—then there is no case from externalities for either compulsory schooling or the governmental financing of schooling. There may, of course, still be a case, on paternalistic or redistributive grounds, for governmental assistance to pay for schooling children of indigent parents, but not for increased government financing of schooling.

In terms of the logic of West's argument, the issue I have raised is implicitly bypassed in the assumption that "each family has a nonzero marginal rate of substitution between another family's consumption of education and each good it consumes itself." My argument is that this rate of substitution is a function of the percentage of the population schooled and the level of schooling; that it may be nonzero and positive for low percentages and low levels but may be zero or even negative for high percentages and high levels; and, more concretely, that it is indeed zero or negligible for percentages and levels that are almost sure to be exceeded in a strictly private system of educational provision.

This distinction between marginal and average externalities is related to, but is not the same as, the distinction between true technical externalities and transfers, which vitiates almost all arguments for government finance of higher schooling from supposed externality considerations.[1]

The distinction is relevant to a large range of issues outside of schooling. For example, it is often argued that government should subsidize basic research because the producer of such research cannot charge for its use; hence there is a net external benefit. But suppose other motives (eleemosynary, emulative, or whatever) lead to private subsidization of basic research (through foundations, privately supported universities, etc.). Does it necessarily follow that there remain *marginal* net positive externalities?

Notes

1. See M. Friedman, "The Higher Schooling in America," *The Public Interest* (11) Spring, 1968: 108-112.

Response to Friedman: Whither Friedman Vouchers?

E.G. West

In my essay I referred to two conventional economic arguments for intervention in education: one, the protection of minors; and two, the argument about external benefits. To this I added the third argument that because of capital market imperfections there was need for the government to provide some kind of loan system to enable families using lower education to borrow from their lifetime income streams. Friedman agrees with the first, disagrees with the second, and presumably does not disagree with the third since he makes no objection to it. In this response I want to develop an idea that was indicated in my essay: that the externalities argument is interdependent with that of capital market imperfection. An elaboration of this point will have an important bearing not only on the present problem of constitutional obstacles to "aid" to nonpublic schools, but also on the status of Friedman's own celebrated voucher scheme. In addition it will, I think, take care of his fear that there has been a "flaw" lurking hitherto around our common arguments.

Like many people, I have in the past benefited considerably from the challenging and constructive influence of Friedman. Perhaps it is not surprising that I need little persuasion about the matter of externalities that he now raises—indeed that I reached the same conclusion ten years ago in my *Education and the State*! Chapter 15 of that book expressed Friedman's present analysis but in less technical language. Reproduction here might help current readers. My argument was as follows:

. . . proof of external economies from schooling is only a necessary, not a sufficient, condition for state financial provision. Such proof does not simultaneously demonstrate that people will privately underinvest in schooling. It may be helpful to illustrate this point from another sphere, that of health.

Suppose that medical research has established the probability that if the average person eats one orange per month he will benefit, not only himself, but also other persons in his environment. For example, research may have indicated that he is much less likely to be the carrier of certain infectious diseases if he consumes oranges at the rate of one per month. What is the relevance of such findings for government policy? Clearly much depends upon established consumption habits. If people are on average already eating two oranges per month then nothing further is to be gained from government intervention. If on the other hand people are consuming on average *one* orange every other month there is a *prima facie* case for some government intervention.[1]

Similarly, private consumption of education may be sufficiently large to

94

call for no further intervention by government. Friedman makes his own subjective judgment not only concerning the existence of average external benefits but also that private interest alone would lead to 90 percent of the population receiving elementary schooling. I wish to add that precise judgment is made difficult because we must envisage not only a full removal of government finance from education but also a dramatic reduction of taxes. Some estimate must be made of the reduction of each individual family's tax burden. I contend that the particular estimates in Tables 1 and 2 (pages 13 and 25) would support Friedman's conclusion in the following sense: most families would be potentially able to finance such minimum schooling if they had access to their lifetime incomes. Whether they would be *willing* to do so without compulsory laws must be yet another subjective judgment.

It will now be asked why, if I had so long ago spotted what Friedman now calls a "flaw" in the conventional argument on externalities, I still persist in using it in the present analysis? My first response is that I do not think the word "flaw" is quite accurate. Friedman's own comment seems to acknowledge that the question is largely a matter of individual *judgment*. He agrees in fact in the idea of externality, because he feels he will be better off than he would be if the fraction schooled at each level were markedly smaller. In other words, he agrees at least that there are *average* external benefits. But the *net* externality depends upon the amount of schooling already being received privately. He argues that he has never found any *plausible* argument for net positive externalities that would not be satisfied if 90 percent received elementary schooling (the three R's). But this, to repeat, is Friedman's personal *judgment*. It happens to be a judgment with which I agree. Nevertheless what is judged plausible for one person may be implausible for another; I think it is too strong to describe differences of opinion on these empirical matters as a "flaw" in the argument.

My historical researches certainly convince me that over 90 percent of individuals in England and in New York State were receiving elementary schooling in the three R's on the eve of government intervention to provide free compulsory education.[2] In my essay I was prepared to grant that *other* people may have different judgments about what people would do in the twentieth century if there were no public school system. I proceeded to use the rubric of externalities, first because it is well established in the literature.[3] second because the Supreme Court's arguments seem to presume such a framework. In addition, I started with the externalities as a useful point of departure. It is common practice in economics to use transitional models to develop the analysis, even though those same models are eventually discarded at the end of the process. In fact, in my essay the externalities argument *is* gradually eroded to the extent that eventually there is nothing but *average* externalities, if at all, in the end.

It will be helpful here to explain this more explicitly and to attempt to present Friedman's valid distinction between marginal and average externalities still more clearly. In Figure 2 the private demand for postsecondary education for family j is shown by the curve D_j. If there were no intervention and if tax collection remained the same, family j would purchase OM units. Assume that government is first prompted to intervene, not from capital market imperfections, but from arguments of external benefits. Because of the external benefits, production of schooling for j can be described in terms of joint supply of output; a unit of education simultaneously satisfies both private and community demand. The community demand (for external benefits) is shown in Figure 2 as D_k. The optimal solution is to extend consumption until the vertical sum of the demand prices, shown as ΣD_1 in the diagram, is equal to the marginal cost, MC, at output Q_1. The two separate demand prices, and therefore public/private cost shares at this consumption, are P_c (the price to the community) and P_f (the price to the family). The sum of these two prices equals the total per-unit cost of $P_c + P_f = OB$. If, in contrast, the parties were to act independently, they would each adjust suboptimally until their *separate* marginal evaluations equalled marginal cost. Notice that the community pays a price P_c that is equal not to the average, but to the *marginal* external benefits. The average benefits, of course, are higher than the marginal ones.

The "flaw" that Friedman speaks of is the assumption that the position and slope of D_k are inevitably similar to those illustrated in Figure 2. This is not so; or at least it has never been proved to be so. Figure 3 shows the same private demand curve D_j and a community demand curve which, though having similar *average* external benefits, reveals zero *marginal* benefits at optimum consumption (Q_2). In this situation members of the community are certainly better off than they would be if family j purchased a significantly smaller schooling. In Friedman's terms, they have benefited from family j's behavior, but, by assumption, they have paid none of the costs. (These externalities are described in the literature as "Pareto-irrelevant.") Incidentally, the probability that marginal external benefits will be zero is increased when there is a presumption that there will be "excessive" expenditure in a private system because private returns from job screening exceed social returns.[4] In other words, if private interest alone could lead to at least Q_2 schooling, then there is no case for externalities for government financing of schooling. Any such financing would amount to pure transfers from users to nonusers.

It is now time to show that a policy conducted on grounds of capital imperfections (my third policy, referred to in the opening paragraph) and policy two (on externalities) are interdependent. Suppose the government policy three resulted in an "unblocking" of the relevant (capital) market, or

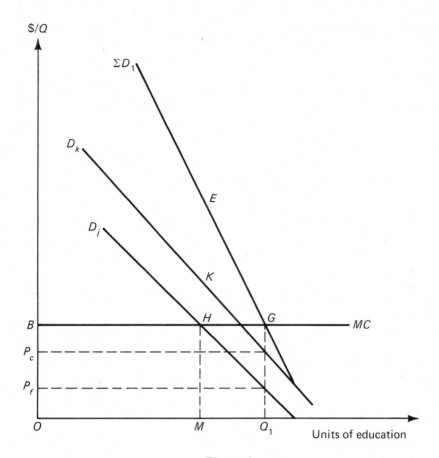

Figure 2

in a modification that made it less "imperfect" for all those reasons explained in my response to Sugarman's essay (page 85). This action will
release funds for the private purchase of more education than before. In
terms of Figures 2 and 3 this would mean a rightward shift in the private
demand curve D_j. The community demand curve D_k would be unaffected.
In Figure 3 this would simply mean extended private purchase beyond Q_2,
the *marginal* external benefits being zero and family j still paying full cost
OB (equal to MC). If, on the other hand, the original configuration of
demand curves were as in Figure 2, and insofar as marginal external
benefits were still positive at the new equilibrium, there would be a new
point of intersection with a new societal demand curve ΣD_2 appearing
farther to the right. This is illustrated in Figure 4, which differs from Figure
2 only in that D_j is farther to the right and consequently so is ΣD (now ΣD_2).

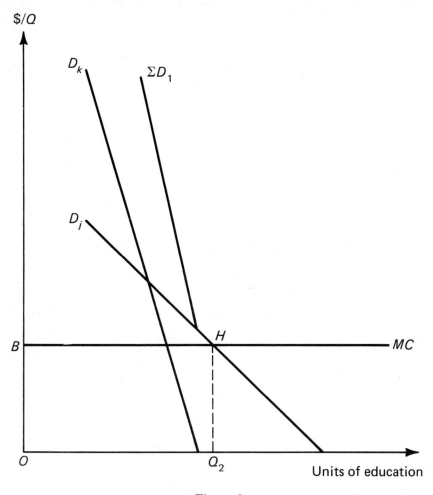

Figure 3

This change brings out an interesting consequence. The public/private cost shares have now changed: the private share increasing and the public share decreasing. The present change from Figure 2 to Figure 4 is a move from a one-third private share of the costs in Figure 2 to a two-thirds share of the costs in Figure 4 (compare P_f in each diagram). It is possible, of course, for the introduction of the government loans scheme to result in a shift of the private demand curve that is sufficient to make the marginal externalities zero. It is this process that I have termed the "erosion" of the externalities argument; and this is the kind of result I was suggesting in my essay. In the end, therefore, marginal externalities *are* zero in my essay, and this conforms with Friedman's present assessment.

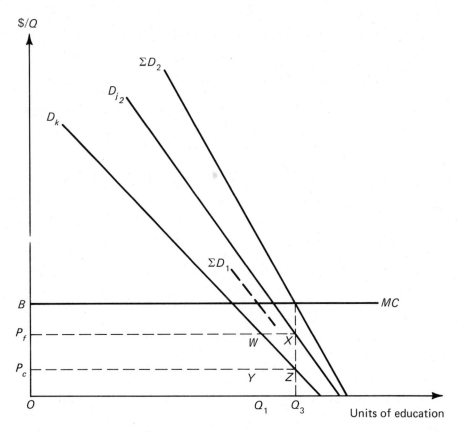

Figure 4

The only possible difference between us is that, without any comment on his part, he may be assuming that the private market would result in zero marginal external benefits even without the help of a government loan scheme. If this is the case, the question may arise to some why Milton Friedman advocated his famous vouchers in the first place? Vouchers require government finance; so why employ them if, as he now believes, families can be expected to produce sufficient *private* finance? His writings I believe contain a logical answer to this question. He separates three levels of issues, first, whether schooling should be compulsory, second, whether it should be governmentally financed or privately financed, third, how it should be *organized*. Friedman's position has always been that whatever may be one's answers on the first two levels, a voucher scheme would produce a better and a more effective organization than the present one; that is vouchers remain a superior alternative to a system of governmentally run as well as financed schools. My own discussion relates mainly to the second of the above levels of issues to which Friedman hitherto has not addressed himself (at least where *lower* education is concerned). I would urge however that the time is now ripe for others to face up to this second question in the same direct manner that Friedman now does; for it is at least as important as the others. More to the point of my essay this question has now become the most urgent of the three because the answer to it has a key bearing on the problem of the Supreme Court's blockage to financial relief of most non-public schools. I detect that, in view of his newly expressed position on external benefits, Milton Friedman's views on the second issue (government or private financing) would be such as to be in favour of an ever larger element of user-prices than that which I am advocating—in which case the relief to parochial schools would be even more pronounced.

All three levels of issues are surely interdependent, and one's position on one of them separately is not sufficient; it is made much more comprehensive and clear if equal analysis of judgment has been applied almost simultaneously to the other two. The last two issues moreover begin to converge in one particular area: the search for the full definition or meaning of 'voucher'. On current definitions the question of who pays for them is left rather loose. I maintain that as we probe for a fuller description of them, the more it will be revealed how much the individual 'recipients' are contributing to their own finance from their own *life-time* taxes. My argument on capital markets can largely reinstate the vouchers in the sense of loans, as discussed in my response to Sugarman. Moreover I am sure that Milton Friedman will agree that the argument of enabling families to purchase from their lifetime incomes considerably strengthens his presumption that marginal externalities will be zero. He would also agree, I am sure, that government intervention on these lines is primarily financial not educational. It follows that this distinction, once made explicit, would enable the government to channel finance to families for educational purposes without violating the First Amendment.

Finally, consider the case in diagrammatic terms where the community demand curve dominates the private demand curve D_j to the extent that the whole of the education is being paid for by the community (a free education system). If a loan system is now introduced, it will shift the private demand curve to the right such that public/private cost shares will change from zero private and 100 percent public, to something that is above a zero direct payment for the private participant and something that is less than a 100 percent payment for the community "partner". This is a situation where the introduction of some elementary loan scheme accompanies the introduction of my user tax; the one policy implies or "justifies" the other.

Notes

1. E.G. West, *Education and the State*, Institute of Economic Affairs, London, 1965, page 226.

2. See E.G. West, *Education and the Industrial Revolution,* Gage, Canada 1975; E.G. West, 'The Political Economy of American Public School Legislation, *Journal of Law and Economics,* 1967.

3. See especially Mark V. Pauly, "Mixed Public and Private Financing of Education," *American Economic Review,* 57(1): March 1967.

4. Joseph E. Stiglitz, "The Theory of Screening," *American Economic Review,* 65(3): June 1975.

Total Reform: Nothing Less

Murray N. Rothbard

West's paper is a valuable admonition to advocates of school vouchers that the voucher plan may well be unconstitutional in the light of the Supreme Court's *Nyquist* decision. Seeking another, constitutional, means to relieve hard-hit private schools, West suggests a move toward full-cost pricing of public schools, thereby relieving both parochial and other private schools from the intolerable burden of competing with subsidized free public schools, and private school parents from the burden of paying twice for education. Hopefully, West's analysis will lead to a reevaluation of the voucher scheme and to a long-needed consideration of the idea of moving toward an educational system that will be free from governmental control and governed solely by the choices of parents on the free market.

Having said this, I must also point out that West's conclusions do not go far enough, and that, still more important, his analysis is deeply flawed. The central flaw is his basic assumption that it is possible for an economist *qua* value-free economist to offer public policy conclusions. On the contrary, it is illegitimate for an economist, or for anyone else, to offer policy conclusions without also introducing ethical propositions from political philosophy.

Before turning to the flaws of West's analysis, I should point out that his conclusions do not go far enough. Why introduce full-cost pricing for public schools only for marginal *increases* in costs? Why not for all school costs? Furthermore, why not stop at the splendid first phase of West's plan—the abolition of each state's public school system—without reintroducing that system a few months later on a "significantly financed" user basis? The abolition of the public school system would be (1) constitutional, (2) relieve the double burden of private school parents, (3) yield full-cost pricing for all schools, (4) ensure genuine competition between every school, and (5) result in free parental choice and a school system governed solely by such choices. It would also provide for all the values of diversity mentioned by West.

Another problem with West's program is his call for a government-guaranteed tuition loan system to tap the student's lifetime earnings. If such a loan system were economic, then it would be provided on the free market by private banks and lending agencies. If private agencies do not supply such tuition loans, then they do not do so because of the high costs of such individual loans, or because of the high risk of default; in either case, there is no good reason for the taxpayer to be forced to subsidize such costly or risky loans. West's optimistic view that such loans would be a "revolving fund" out of which everyone in a sense pays for his/her own education ignores differences of time preference between individuals, as well as the fact that childless adults would be forced to pay permanently for the education of others without drawing from such a "fund." West's reference to the capital or loan market as being "imperfect" simply smuggles in the illegitimate standard of "perfect competition"; in reality, there are, and can be, no "perfect" markets, and the economic world would be a shambles if they should ever exist!

West's criticism of the *Nyquist* decision is also largely beside the point. While West is correct in criticizing the Court's identification of tax credits as equivalent to a subsidy, the remainder of his criticism is flawed by his attempt to criticize *as a pure economist* a decision in political philosophy. The First Amendment criterion of avoiding state entanglement in religion is, in my view, a correct and important one, and the *Nyquist* decision is perfectly within such a framework. Nowhere does West meet or attempt to criticize such a criterion head-on, as indeed he cannot if he avoids political philosophy. He is also incorrect in his apparent definition of "established" as simply an existing institution, as well as in his misconception that the founding fathers were only concerned with opposing an establishment of religion by a "nondemocratic monarchic regime." On the contrary, the founding fathers were concerned with abolishing all state support of religion, be it monarchic or "democratic," as is evidenced by the numerous states which abolished their own religious establishment in the years following the American Revolution.

Also deeply fallacious is West's repeated identification of religious and general education with the joint supply problem of hides and beef on the free market. What he fails to understand is that the concept of "subsidy" only applies to the state and not to the free market, and therefore correctly applies to state aid to education but not to consumer choice on the beef and hide markets. If the consumers spend $100 million on the products of firm A, this is not a "subsidy"; on the other hand, if the government does so, it *is* a subsidy. Again we are back in the basic political philosophy of the founding fathers: namely, that it is immoral and illegitimate for the government to subsidize individual firms or industries, thereby going beyond the ideal of equality before the law to confer "special privileges" on particular firms by money obtained from the taxpayers.

To turn to the essentials of West's analytic schema, it suffers from two fundamental fallacies: (1) identifying legislative action with the alleged views of the "median voter," and (2) more importantly, attempting to make valuefree policy conclusions on behalf of government-supported education by using the "normative" concept of externalities. On the first point, West finds himself able to support some form of aid to parochial schools by invoking the alleged values of the "median voter" of New York

State, as supposedly embodied in the state legislature's measures to provide such aid. Now, in the first place, even if the median voter did hold such values, it would be illegitimate for West to simply ratify such values in the guise of a "valuefree" economist obeying the will of the voter. Suppose, for example, that the median voter of New York State favored the immediate incarceration of all Roman Catholics; would West feel constrained to ratify *such* values as well, and if not, why not? And if this seems a far-fetched example, then it should be noted that many observers of public opinion hold that a large majority of the voting public would no longer, if asked, vote to ratify the First Amendment or the remainder of the Bill of Rights. Does that mean that all these hard-won rights and freedoms should be scrapped? If not, why not?

But second, the identification of legislative action with the median voter is a highly naive view of how representative government really operates. Voters are never permitted to make such direct choices; voters cast their choices once every two or four years between two candidates, each of whom presents a vague, complex package of programs (usually virtually identical), which he or she is not pledged to fulfill during the term of office—and usually does not fulfill. The voters of New York State have never spoken directly on the issue of aid to parochial schools. The state legislature votes by responding to the lobbying of special pressure and interest groups. Indeed, the action of the state legislature in this case is far more likely to have been responsive to the median Roman Catholic priest than to the median voter.

We come now to West's central fallacy: his use of alleged "externalities" to justify, as a valuefree economist, government provision or support for education. The assusumption, never supported or analyzed by West, is that one person's education benefits everyone else in society, and that the other people should therefore be forced to pay for such benefits. There are numerous vital fallacies in this approach which West does not consider, much less attempt to justify.

In the first place, even if such external benefits existed, there is no way to measure them monetarily. How do we know whether tax-supported funding for education exceeds, or indeed falls below, such alleged benefits? As a corollary point, since individual utilities, benefits, and costs are purely subjective, they can never be measured or estimated, and hence West's apparatus of "community demand curves," social "marginal cost," etc., is totally illegitimate. There *are no* community demand curves or social costs and benefits even conceptually, let alone in practice: the only demand is that revealed in the market by explicit and voluntary consumer purchases (and even here we know only the quantity demanded at any point of time and not the shape of the curve itself.)

Second, externalities of education may well be negative, and not positive; certainly, if we confine ourselves to the alleged value freedom of economics, we must then conclude that even if *one* person suffers negative external effects from someone else's education, then it is illegitimate, and goes beyond the economist's province, to override *his/her* net negative effects by forcing him/her to submit to other people's net positive effects. Furthermore, since all costs and benefits are subjective to each individual, it is conceptually impossible to sum up these costs and benefits into some notion of "net" positive or negative effects.

Third, let us consider the various possible forms of net *negative* effect from someone else's education, and we will see the scope of the problem.

(1) Some people might feel that the education of other people is *evil*; e.g., the Amish, who are opposed to education, may well suffer net negative effects from others' education.

(2) The idea of education as evil is not as far-fetched as it might first appear. Witness the current controversy over sex education in the schools. A substantial number of parents feel that sex education outside of the home is evil, and hence suffer severe negative externalities from such education. Witness also the current West Virginia controversy over textbooks in the public schools; whichever way the origin of humans or of language may be taught, for example, whether from the secular or the Fundamentalist point of view, numerous parents will suffer negative external effects from such teaching.

(3) Some people, such as the late Albert Jay Nock, may hold that many, if not most, children in society are *in*educable, and therefore that government support of education, in providing schooling for a mass of *in*educable people, injures not only the rest of society but also the children themselves. In short, government support of education leads to mal-investment in education, and a mass of "overeducated" and miseducated children, who would have benefited both themselves and others by working instead. In recent years, such educational theorists as Paul Goodman have made similar points using very different rhetoric (e.g., uninterested, unhappy "working-class" children are forced or induced into an environment dominated by "middle-class values").

(4) The externalities argument proves too much, for education in its "widest" sense consists of far more than formal schooling. People learn far more from books, newspapers, TV, friends, and parents than they do from formal schooling. On the West model, then, the positive externalities from everyone's having wise parents, hobnobbing with wise and intelligent friends, and reading "proper" literature and newspapers is far greater than from going to school. The same is true, in reverse, of the substantial negative externalities which we all suffer from others having bad parents,

improper friends, reading the wrong papers and books, etc. Shouldn't West, as a valuefree welfare economist, therefore advocate that the government tax everyone in order to supply everyone with the proper newspapers, books, friends, and parents? Shouldn't he advocate government supply, or at least support, of newspapers, books, and even parents? And shouldn't he go further and advocate the compulsory provision of wise friends, parents, etc., and the outlawry of the bad ones? And if not, why not?

(5) West completely neglects the substantial negative effects of taxation, including the opportunity cost of the various uses on which the taxed subjects would have spent their money. Furthermore, he ignores the net negative external effects of such government action on those libertarians in society who oppose all taxation and government activity, above and beyond their own payment of taxes. Where do these people count in the valuefree panoply of welfare economics?

(6) West makes only one brusque attempt to support the concept of positive externalities from education: that crime will be reduced by the provision of education, and that everyone is interested in the reduction of crime. But, apart from the other criticisms mentioned above, what support is there for this common but totally unfounded hypothesis? As John O. Nelson has shown elsewhere, the statistical correlations are certainly the other way round. As education has continued to increase in the modern world, the crime rate has increased as well. While this does not prove causation, it certainly provides considerable evidence *against* the idea that education reduces crime. Furthermore, Nelson has offered various theoretical considerations to maintain that education in fact *increases* crime. Suppose this were ture; would West *then* advocate not only the abolition of the public school system, and of all government support to education, but also active government discouragement and penalizing of education? Again, if not, why not?

In addition to Nelson's philosophical reasons, incidentally, there is one practical support for the view that education and literacy *increase* crime. An educated person *can* commit all the crimes that are committed by the uneducated; but education provides the means to commit many crimes that are simply beyond the reach of the illiterate and uneducated (e.g., forgery, embezzlement, electronic bugging). Otheer things being equal, then, this addition to capacity will tend to increase crime among the educated.

It should not be thought that West's flaws and fallacies are unique; on the contrary, they are endemic to modern welfare economics. The unanalyzed assumptions, the deeply flawed reliance on externalities, the objectification of social costs and benefits, the unsupported assumption of net benefits from education, the use of unrealistic standards of "perfection," and, above all, the neglect of political philosophy and the attempt to arrive at political conclusions *qua* economist, are central to what is wrong with welfare economics today. The essence of the problem is that economists want to have their cake and eat it too: they want desperately to take stands on public policy, yet at the same time to preserve their "scientific" mantle of valuefree economics, free from the controversial and emotionally charged problems of political philosophy. But this cannot be done; to be truly valuefree, economics must purge itself of all the fallacious assumptions of its "welfare" branch; but then it will become clear to all economists that to make policy conclusions, they cannot escape the adopting of a coherent, ethical political philosophy.

Response to Rothbard: Half a Loaf is Better Than None

E.G. West

It is obviously now necessary to make fully explicit some of the more important of the basic "rules and assumptions of the game" in the present discussion—rules and assumptions that I was accepting *implicitly*, and that I believe most other commentators have been accepting. I was assuming a given constitution of the American form, that is, a constitution that embodies, or at least aspires to, the system of checks and balances and the separation of powers—a system that has been written about for over three centuries. One of the important "pillars" of this constitution that I was assuming without question is, of course, the First Amendment. Rothbard objects that nowhere do I attempt to examine its criterion head-on. When and if I were to do so, moreover, he insists that my economics would necessarily become inextricably mixed with political philosphy. True, I did not express a value judgment for or against the First Amendment. I was assuming the constitution to be *given*, and that my personal views concerning it were irrelevant. I still uphold this position; but if Rothbard is still curious about my own values, he may now find satisfaction in my second essay that involves what I still believe to be the *separate* issue of political philosophy (see the new essay in this volume, "The Philosophical and Historical Interpretation of the First Amendment," on pages 147-153).

Rothbard objects in particular that I do not criticize the criterion of avoiding state entanglement in religion. The word "entanglement," however, is not contained in the original statute. It is part of the new judicial currency of language developed from recent Supreme Court decisions. But I *did* meet this concept head-on; I maintained that the notion of entanglement is not a very helpful one. I argued this in the context of my joint supply model where I observed that, in the parallel case of beef and hides, the production of the one commodity (service) is *inextricably* "entangled" with the production of the other. This did not mean, however, that the purchasers of the one commodity (service) were subsidizing the purchasers of the other. And I cannot find any meaning in Rothbard's argument that a subsidy is *whatever* a government spends. (Are public expenditures on roads and defense *subsidies?*) Rothbard may have deep objections to my joint supply model (and I shall come to these in a moment), but he cannot argue that I did not face the whole new legal notion of "entanglement."

Rothbard himself expresses explicitly strong value judgments in support of the First Amendment. I presume he similarly champions the other main features of the American constitution: the separation of powers and the rule of law. Within this framework there are explicit sets of individual rights requiring protection. The state that emerges can be viewed in two dimensions, with the first relating to the constitutional stage and the second to the postconstitutional stage. These are: (1) the protective state, and (2) the productive state.[1] The first is the prior enforcing agency or institution that is charged with the responsibility of upholding agreed-upon rights and voluntarily negotiated contracts. The second is the agency for financing or providing collective or public goods. One of the most important rights enforced by the protective state is the right to freedom from arbitrary arrest. Each individual has the right to liberty provided she or he does not impinge on that of others. The legal or protective state must ideally be neutral in all its actions. Moreover, this state (unlike the productive state) is *not* a decision-making body. It is not concerned with producing "the social good" or some community ideal that transcends the individual members. The protective state has no legislating function or process through which individuals in the community choose collectively rather than privately. It is through the later, productive state, that individuals legislate for themselves public goods (such as education, defense, and roads). The legislative bodies themselves are subject to the wider laws of the state, laws that are enforced by the primary protective state.

Consider, now, and in the above framework, Rothbard's question of whether I would feel constrained to ratify values such as those revealed when the median voter of New York State favored the immediate incarceration of all Roman Catholics. Apart from the irrelevance of my personal values, such a question is out of order, for I take it for granted that we are participating in a debate, the rules of which include the assumption of a republican, written constitution described above. In such a situation the postconstitutional or productive state would *not have authority to incarcerate Roman Catholics*, and not even if there were a substantial majority of voters in favor of doing so. Roman Catholics, like other citizens, possess the rights to be free from arbitrary arrest and to enjoy the rule of law. Similarly it does *not* follow that a large voting majority at the level of the postconstitutional productive state has the right to scrap what Rothbard calls hard-won rights and freedoms. I am surprised that he did not interpret my own argument to assume respect to all these parts of the Constitution. By similar reasoning, we should strongly question whether forcing religious families to pay twice for their education is paying proper respect to the "hard-won" rights and freedoms enshrined in the First Amendment, for that constitutional "pillar" offered protection to religions in the sense that they were to be free from discriminatory treatment by governments. Rothbard should ask himself whether these hard-won freedoms have not already been scrapped in this case of religious activity. Nowhere does *he* meet head-on this important point, the point I have been striving to emphasize throughout. And it is for this reason that I firmly reject his conclusion that the *Nyquist* decision is perfectly within the framework of the First Amendment. This is not a matter of personal values; it is a verdict about consistency and logic in constitutional interpretation.

Next consider Rothbard's view that it is a fallacy to identify legislative action with the views of the median voter. He claims that it is illegitimate for me, in the guise of a "valuefree" economist, to ratify the values expressed by such a voter. I agree, but I did *not* so ratify. I simply took the wishes of the median voter as a *datum* from which the analysis could begin. I expressed no personal views of whether my own preferences coincided with those of the median voter. I set out to "predict" a policy that would be politically successful in the sense that the median voter's wishes would be respected. This is different from prescribing policy, that is, urging a new program on the grounds of *my* normative judgment. I did not suggest that the median voter's preferences were of "dictatorial" importance. They are always constrained by those wider laws that provide the checks and balances mentioned earlier. In the *Nyquist* case, in fact, the median voter's preferences had conspicuously to meet a constitutional "obstacle" in the form of the Supreme Court deliberation. The Court had to decide what is and what is not "aid" to parochial schools in order to make an attempt to safeguard the spirit of the First Amendment. I argued that their reasoning happened to be wrong in this case. It was strongly colored by the particular fiscal pattern under which prevailing governments operate. As James Buchanan observes, when taxes are plausibly "general," there is normally no "constitutional" basis for minority objection, regardless of the distribution of benefit, or of the nonvoluntariness of the decision.[2] Because of a fiscal pattern based on plausible "general" taxes, the United States courts have, in my assessment, failed to acknowledge much discrimination. The courts give too much weight to the need to demonstrate *overt* discrimination. But, to meet its demands, the more that the fiscal pattern can be switched from general to specific taxes on specific individuals, the more the discrimination *can be made* overt. A switch from property taxes and sales taxes toward more reliance on user taxes would be a movement of this kind. I do not, as Rothbard interprets me, "support some form of aid to parochial schools." What emerges from my analysis is not a proposal for "aid" but the argument that the present public school system is involved in hostility to religion, an outcome that the First Amendment forbids.

With respect to the rather tedious question of who exactly is the median voter, we may postulate all kinds of models of democracy. It does not dispose of my argument to assert that I was implying an "ideal" democratic form in which voters make constant and direct choices. The voters' choices may be periodic and indirect; yet they still remain voters; and they still have *some* influence. Indeed, I would go further than Rothbard in qualifying the ideal model as representative of the real world. The roles of voters are limited largely to the selection of representatives who are persons from their own ranks. The representatives then participate in legislative and executive decision making. Certainly it is they who then make the *direct* and final choices on budget allocations and so on. But the representatives themselves have personal preferences about particular patterns and sizes of public sector outlays; for this reason alone budgetary results will not fully reflect voters' preferences. The politician has considerable freedom for choosing his own preferred position. At the same time this does not mean we should ignore the fact that he is constrained by voters indirectly through prospects for reelection.

Again while one must acknowledge also that the bureaucracy itself is a political constituency that can influence final outcome, all this means is that the ordering of voters is not what it seems at first sight, and that some voters have, in effect, more voting power than others. This does not deny that an ordered set of voters does exist, and that any decision rule based on simple majority voting must satisfy the preferences of the median voter within this qualified set if it is to succeed. Now, allowing for all the above kinds of ''imperfections'' in the political process, I would still find it very difficult to believe, as Rothbard does, that in the *Nyquist* situation the case is "far more likely to have been responsive to the median Roman Catholic priest than to the median voter." If the Catholic priest was in such a commanding position, it is difficult to see why the quantities of aid incorporated in the New York legislation were of such modest amounts, amounts that fell very far short of stopping Catholic parents from paying twice for their education. Indeed, if the priest *was* so influential, why should we not expect the political advocacy of a system that so heavily subsidized Catholic schools that public school users were the ones that paid twice? In fact, this did not occur; for this reason I think it reasonable to assume that the ''key'' median voter was more representative of non-Catholics and of the public-school-using class.

One must not forget that in the *Nyquist* situation the *public school users sought to gain benefits from the legislation.* As explained in the preamble to the New York statutes, the public school users faced impoverishment of their own educational system by the movement into it of ''refugees'' from bankrupt parochial schools. After the collapse of parochial schools, the public school user not only would have suffered overcrowded classes but would have lost entirely the indirect subsidy from the nonpublic school user. In these circumstances it is understandable that public school users were willing to "sacrifice" *some* of this subsidy to enable parochial schools to survive, for this would prevent an even bigger "sacrifice" from being imposed on them.

Of all the alleged shortcomings in my analysis, Rothbard believes that my use of the externalities concept is the most serious. This criticism is not confined to me but (as he admits) ambitiously takes on the whole of modern welfare economics. He claims that there are no community demand curves or social costs and benefits even conceptually. This claim challenges all the economist pioneers of modern public goods literature from Paul Samuelson to James Buchanan. Now without the public goods analysis it seems impossible to explain the private production of "collective" goods, such as the common facilities provided by local sports clubs or the general facilities like landscape gardens and recreational facilities of condominium projects. It is clear that the individual members of these "clubs" have a schedule of various personal demands for these services corresponding with various prices for them. It is obvious, too, that such demands can be aggregated or vertically summed (as in Figure 1). Rothbard claims that the only demand is that revealed in the market by explicit and voluntary consumer purchases. Yet the demand for private club facilities *is* revealed in the market; it follows from explicit and voluntary consumer behavior. It is only an extension of this same reasoning to argue that some collective goods can reasonably be purchased through one particular "club" institution, namely, government.

Rothbard seems to want to avoid acknowledging externalities unless they are negative. He cannot have it both ways. If he wants to insist that externalities are negative, he has to admit they exist. Moreover he has to face his own question how they are to be measured. I am not at all disturbed by his proposition that empirically externalities *are* negative. Indeed I could add to his list of examples. If externalities are *typically* negative, all this would mean in terms of Figure 1 is that the community demand curve (D_k) cuts below the origin at the private equilibrium OM. The point on the aggregate demand curve (ΣD) corresponding with OM education would now be *below* the MC curve. Since the social optimal position would be where the ΣD curve cuts the MC curve, *less* education would be required. In this case the members of the community would be "purchasing," up to a point, *reductions* in private education. The question now arises of where the "typical" community demand curve lies. It is certainly true that we usually aggregate positive and negative individual demands in the D_k curve. Rothbard argues that if we confine ourselves to valuefree economics, we must conclude that even if *one* person suffers negative external effects from someone else's education, it is as illegitimate to override his/her net negative effects by forcing him/her to submit to other people's net positive effects. But this can be expressed the other way round. If some persons enjoy positive external effects from someone else's education, then is it not illegitimate to override *his/her* net positive effects by preventing him/her from internalizing them in cooperation with others? This brings us to inescapable conflicts within the democratic setting, and it is here that we bring into focus and make explicit another "rule of the game." If Rothbard is still operating within the rubric of a republican constitution, he reveals the major flaw in his analysis when he treats in isolation the rights of individuals to use private property without any constraint. The fact is that these rights cannot be treated in isolation from those rights which are indirectly represented by membership in a collectivity that is constitutionally empowered to make decisions under predetermined rules.[3] Therefore, in determining our community demand curve for external benefits, the productive state pays special respect to the demand of the majority. Postconstitutional injury to some need not tie the hands of government. Rich people suffer negative effects (injuries) from progressive income taxes. It does not follow that such tax structure indicates "illegitimate welfare economics." Of course some may argue that, by the same token, it is not illegitimate to force some people to pay twice for their education. This does *not* follow however. The majority does not in this case enjoy special rights to disproportionate taxes because they are largely religious minorities; and their rights have been explicitly and previously protected by the Constitution's First Amendment. I am perplexed that Rothbard does not see this full "libertarian" significance of the same statute.

I am fully willing to agree with the proposition, as I have already pointed out in my response to Friedman, that one can be misled empirically about the existence or degree of external benefits. I must repeat that I do not *personally* support the concept of positive externalities with the argument that crime will be reduced. Nobody needs more persuasion than I do that the evidence does not support it.[4] The point about my use of the externalities concept, to repeat, is that it is a conventional instrument of analysis through which one can *begin* to enter the debate with other participants. Having met them halfway, we can eventually drop the whole apparatus of externalities, and new concepts can take its place.

Since the externalities apparatus *is* largely discarded by the end of my essay, I offered an alternative hypothesis to explain the government presence in education. This was the proposition about capital market imperfections, a proposition that suggests governments intervene to enable people to purchase education from their *lifetime* incomes. Rothbard is not happy with this proposition either. I am sympathetic with his point of view, but I urge him not to jump to conclusions too soon on this issue. He assumed that if there were no intervention, people would be able to purchase education without any financial inconvenience; they would buy education just like they now purchase food and clothing for their children.

We certainly do not have much in the way of empirical knowledge on this issue (although my own historical research indicates that in the nineteenth century the capital market imperfection problem was not as serious as is sometimes assumed). In the twentieth century, however, we may have more doubts on the matter, doubts that lead us to explore whether governments can legitimately provide unusually efficient loan schemes to better enable people to purchase education privately. I can see Rothbard's sensitivity to the word "imperfect" to describe a private capital market. But this is almost a shorthand expression these days. It does not necessarily commit its user to any doctrinaire attachment to state intervention. Nor does it suggest that we can ever reach the state of perfect competition in practice. I am quite willing to consider the possibility that a government-created loan scheme could be more "imperfect" than those attempted by the private market.[5] At the same time, I believe that it is perfectly reasonable to explore the possibility that governments do have a comparative advantage in this field. The biggest "imperfection" in a loan market for education is the propensity of individuals to default. Private lenders face heavy costs in collecting information concerning the lifetime incomes of the borrowers. Governments already possess huge machinery for collection and information purposes in the form of the income tax administration. The marginal costs of using this machinery to implement a government-sponsored loan system could be significantly lower than any private counterpart. It is strongly arguable that the incentives to default on income tax statements are very much lower than those on private financial contracts. This type of government loan scheme has not yet been attempted in higher education, but it is presumptuous to believe that it could *not* be successful. More important, it may not be too fanciful to assume that the present "tax" finance system in education tries to *simulate* a loan system that does use the tax collection machinery and one that gives people access to their lifetime incomes.

What kind of world does Rothbard seek? He says explicitly that it is one of zero intervention in education. Such a world would not force the users of parochial schools to pay twice for their education. A return to it would mean that parochial school users would be better off than they are today. Would he therefore consider this move equivalent to aid to parochial schools? If so, would he regard it as an infringement of the First Amendment? Surely not. Yet if he reads my essay once again, he will see that the argument is pointing substantially in his direction, and it is not based on arbitrary personal value judgments. My essay predicts or outlines a "solution" that is not as revolutionary as Rothbard's, but it would benefit all parties within the realistic assumption that "we start from here" with existing inequalities. Rothbard must come to terms with political realities; he should consider whether half a loaf is not better than none at all.

Notes

1. I borrow this terminology from J.M. Buchanan, *The Limits of Liberty,* University of Chicago Press, 1975, page 68.

2. Ibid., page 104.

3. Ibid., page 73.

4. See E.G. West, *Education and the State,* Institute of Economic Affairs, London, 1970, Chapter 3. This chapter is concerned exclusively with a full refutation of the notion that crime will be reduced with increased education.

5. Indeed, I argue that this is also in the *present system* of loans for *higher* education in America and Canada. See E.G. West, "Student Loan: A Reappraisal," A Report to the Ontario Economic Council, 1976 (Toronto).

School User Taxes and
Economic Efficiency

James M. Buchanan

West proposes the introduction of school user taxes as a means of reducing the cost disparity between parochial and public education. This proposal is offered as a political change which would indirectly improve the financial viability of parochial schools without running afoul of constitutional constraints. In the interesting discussion between West and his critics contained in this volume, many of the problems of implementing West's proposal have been examined. I shall, in this commentary, restrict myself to an examination of West's proposal within the strict confines of welfare economics, and I shall develop an argument that tends to support his proposal on normative efficiency grounds. Somewhat surprisingly, the point which I shall develop here is overlooked in the discussion except in a short passage of Sugarman's paper. Less surprisingly, the point is too often wholly neglected in the more general analysis of governmental financing of education. My comments are devoted to the question of the possible efficiency attributes of school user charges. I shall not be directly concerned either with the plight of the parochial schools or with the constitutional issues that school user taxes or charges might (or might not) create.

There are costs in educating a child, whether these be measured in monetary units or in resources that might be used productively in alternative ways. If education is first considered to be wholly a private consumption service, akin to holiday travel or beer, there would be no efficiency argument for collective or governmental intrusion of any sort into its provision and financing through ordinary market organization. Families with children to be educated would simply purchase the desired services, in their chosen quantity and quality, from competitive and profit-seeking firms willing to supply them. In West's 20-person community, the education of the four children would be paid exclusively by their own families. And, indeed, if this were not the organizational-financing arrangement, economic inefficiencies would emerge. Suppose that we could observe a community in which educational services are known to be purely private consumption services, but which for some reason finances its schools through general taxation, levied on the whole community membership. In such a setting, the family with children is subsidized by others in the community. Issues of equity aside, this subsidy will modify incentives for

Professor Buchanan's participation in this book was invited at a late stage and in the hope that he would write a foreword. After reading the contributions, he was more disposed to join in the fray of the debate! Hence the present piece, and his knowledge of the others.

116

the creation of children. If we assume that family decisions on childbearing are motivated, in part, by economic considerations, the subsidy will have the effect of generating a population that is inefficiently large, other things being equal, with efficiency defined here in orthodox economic terms. Families will not take into account the social cost of educating a child when they make childbearing choices.

From this elementary analysis it follows that, to the extent that education is a private consumption service, some differential pricing or taxing of families with children to be educated will be necessary to secure an optimal adjustment in the number of children to be produced. This is an implicit economic rationale for West's proposal; indeed, in his 20-person community, families with children agree to pay differential shares in school costs in direct relationship to the share of private benefits in the total. West's economic defense of user taxes is based, in part, on the implicit claim that such private family benefits exist and that families should be required to pay differentially for these benefits.

All this is prefatory to my main argument. I suggest here that, quite apart from private consumption benefits to the family, there is an efficiency argument which may be adduced for the implementation of user charges. That is to say, even if there should be no private consumption benefits, even if all the benefits from education are captured under the familiar externality rubric, there is still an efficiency basis for placing differential taxes on the families who have children. My argument here is based directly on an extension of Thompson's analysis of taxation and national defense.[1]

Consider a setting at the other end of the private-public goods spectrum. Assume now that there are *no* private family benefits from education, that the only social benefits are those summarized under the traditional externality rubric. (In a practical sense, this would mean that a family would have no more interest in the education of its own child than in the education of any other child in the community and that childless families would have the same overall interest in education as those with children.) In the orthodox theory of public economics (before Thompson) this would seem to be the idealized setting for the application of general-tax financing, with tax shares based somehow on individuals' marginal evaluations of educational services. There would seem to be no place in this scheme for user charges, and any tax share scheme that ensures the satisfaction of the familiar Samuelson conditions for public goods provision would seem to generate Pareto-efficient results.

As Thompson has demonstrated with the national defense example, however, the orthodox theory may neglect an important margin of adjustment. Despite the apparently extreme assumption about the absence of private consumption benefits, the subsidization of childbearing emphasized in the earlier model remains. In making a decision to have a child, a family will not take into account the social marginal cost of its offspring. If education is considered to be a necessary investment outlay on the part of the community, because of the presumed externality reasons, it follows that each additional child brought into the community adds a social cost, which must be borne by someone. The orthodox public goods theory looks exclusively at the margin of adjustment in the amount of education to be provided; it completely neglects the margin of adjustment which determines the number of children. Efficiency requires that both margins be adjusted optimally, and this strongly suggests that families confronted with childbearing choices be required to take into account the genuine social costs of their actions. Differential user charges or taxes may, therefore, be implied, despite the absence of differential benefits.

Under these extreme conditions, the differential user tax on families with school-age children would run squarely into distributional objections, much stronger than those which West encountered with his more limited, and seemingly more defensible, proposal. Can the imposition of differential school user taxes or charges be supported on pure efficiency grounds, quite apart from distributional objections?

To answer this question fully, it becomes necessary to place the whole user charge discussion in a Coase-theorem context.[2] The efficiency argument for the imposition of user charges in the pure externality model, as sketched above, depends upon an implicit assumption about the existing structure of property rights in the community, an assumption that may be disputed. If potential childbearers are presumed, from the outset, to have no right to bring additional children into the world unless they bear the full social marginal costs of so doing, the efficiency argument traced out above follows directly. Let us suppose, however, that the existing structure of rights, as understood and commonly interpreted, gives potential childbearers the right to have children without undergoing the marginal social costs. Or, conversely, suppose that other members in the community do not have the rights to their nominally held claims independently of the rights of others to impose these costs against such claims.

Under the assumptions of the Coase theorem, income effects aside, the same allocative outcome would be efficient under either of the two divergent "property rights" arrangements. But the institutional means of reaching efficiency may well be quite different in the two cases. With the second structure of rights—that in which families do possess rights to produce children without paying the social marginal costs (defined in conventional terms)—the child-producing margin must be brought into optimal adjustment as before; but it cannot, in this case, be accomplished by the imposition of differential user taxes or charges. What is required here is that those who are potentially damaged—other members of the community—must "bribe" families into refraining from having more than the efficient number of children. Institutionally, this might be secured by the general-tax financing of education, along with general-tax financing of some explicit subsidies to women of childbearing age who remain free of pregnancy. (Such a proposal was at one time recommended for India by Stephen Enke.)

This might be observed in the pure externality model, where there are no private family benefits from education. If we allow for some mix between private family benefits and generalized benefits to the community, efficiency might still require user taxes of the variety proposed by West. Where does this leave us in assessing alternative structures of education finance? Once we allow for a recognition that the child-producing margin exists and that economic considerations influence child-producing decisions, economic efficiency requires that user charges in some form be observed, or that bribes of some sort akin to those outlined above be present, or that some mixture of both be in existence. The child-producing margin cannot be optimally adjusted in the absence of both user charges for education (or for child-producing generally) and bribes for not producing children. These alternatives span the possible ranges of rights.

It seems likely that many of the distributional objections to user charges for schools are based, implicitly, on the presumption that rights to produce children are inviolate, regardless of the marginal social costs. The right to a "free public education," noted by Freeman, can be interpreted as an aspect of this implicit structure. At the least, the discussion suggests that there is far from any consensus, either among lawyers or among others, on just what the existing structure of rights is. There is considerable ambiguity here, and it becomes, in some final stage, a function of the judiciary to make a determination. In one structure, there is a clear efficiency argument for the introduction of school user charges, or taxes. In the other, there is an efficiency argument for the introduction of subsidies for not producing children. Because of the ambiguities here, either of these policy stances might be supported. But it would be inconsistent to oppose both of these alternatives.[a]

Where does this analysis leave us when we come to West's primary emphasis, which was that of offering a constitutional means of assisting parochial schools? To the extent that the externality argument for education continues to dominate the political discussion of financing, and to the extent that user taxes of the sort West proposes are rejected, a strong case can be made for the introduction of subsidies for not producing children.

---

[a]This is not to suggest that judicial delineation of rights, even if made explicit, need be internally consistent. As my colleague Robert Staaf has noted, the rights to produce children may be adjudged "inalienable," and hence not subject to "purchase" through bribes or subsidies for not having children. At the same time, however, courts might hold that the imposition of direct school user charges violates parents' rights to "free" schooling. In this setting, where "trade" is impossible, economic efficiency loses its elementary meaning.

But the net efficiency gain generated by such a policy would itself do nothing at all toward improving the lot of the parochial schools. Indirectly, however, any policy proposal or discussion that calls attention to the decisions of families to produce children, on the child-producing margin of adjustment, might tend to cause pressures to be brought to bear toward the introduction of at least nominal differential charges or taxes on school users. This implicit assignment of property rights is consistent with the "polluter pays" principle, one that is often supported by economists in other contexts. And, as pollution and congestion generally become more significant social problems, are conceived to be so by the public, and are related directly to population size, the argument for looking at the structure of property rights in a way that would support the efficiency argument for the imposition of school user charges becomes more and more convincing.

In a frontier society, with population scarcity, there may well exist positive externalities from child-producing that more than offset the costs of public education. In such a setting, the tradition of the "free public school," and the implicit structure of rights involved, might have possessed some efficiency justification. In a mature society, with a population density that guarantees the emergence of congestion and pollution in all its forms, the positive externalities seem to be nonexistent. In this setting, it can, with some plausibility, be claimed that the alternative structure of rights, one that gives the family no rights to produce children without paying the marginal social costs, becomes more "efficient."

Notes

1. Earl A. Thompson, "Taxation and National Defense," *Journal of Political Economy,* 82(July/August 1974): 755-782.

2. The basic analysis is R.H. Coase, "The Problem of Social Cost," *Journal of Law and Economics,* 3(October 1960): 1-44. In sum, the Coase theorem states that, in the absence of transactions costs and on the presumption that exchanges are possible, allocatively efficient results will be attained, regardless of the structure of property rights. Furthermore, the same results will be produced under alternative property rights arrangements provided only that income effects can be neglected. In a normative context, the theorem suggests that the same results should be attained if efficiency is to characterize the system.

Response to Buchanan: School User Taxes and Economic Equity

E.G. West

In his interesting exploration of wider issues of economic theory, Buchanan postulates two polar extremes with two opposite sets of property rights. In the first we have a world where the benefits of education are entirely individual or private. In the second the benefits of education are entirely public (external to the individual). In the latter situation, where education is paid for by the community, the population will be too large because a family will not take into account the social cost of its offspring. But this result, as Buchanan recognizes, depends on the nature of the particular externalities. If children are regarded basically by the rest of society (the "neighbors") as potential threats to property, then society may use free education as one means of conditioning the young population to be less than "naturally" crime-prone. If the provision of education free of charge also encourages marginal increases in the size of families, this second result would certainly be counterproductive to the first, for the larger population will include a larger potential for criminal behavior.

Suppose, however, that the external benefit from education is seen in the form of greater economic growth. Suppose too that population is below the optimum level. The marginal education effects and marginal population effects would now be complementary, as in the case of Buchanan's frontier society. If, however, society *is* interested in increased population, it is not clear why it should select one parental expenditure—education—for special attention. Population can also be affected at the margin by free food, free housing, and free clothing. An interesting question remains why, in the last century, education alone became universally "free." Buchanan suggests that many of the distributional objections by many people to user charges for schools might be based, implicitly, on the assumption that rights to produce children are inviolate, regardless of the marginal social cost. Logically, however, we should see equally intense objection to the continuation of private charges for children's food, clothing, and housing, charges which certainly do negate the idea of an inviolate right to produce children. Because objections are not made so strongly in respect to these other necessities of life, "free education" fails clearly to connect with such absolute rights. My position is reinforced by the historical fact that free education has not been with us from the very beginning; in America and Britain it dates only from about a century ago.

The direction of my remarks reduces the strength of the possible objections to Buchanan's subsidy to encourage smaller families. It is interesting next to conjecture the form that such a subsidy would take. One way would be to provide free schooling to the first or second child but to charge user taxes for the education of, say, the third or fourth child. It is interesting then to compare this efficiency reasoning with the distributional argument of John Coons. Coons was apprehensive about my user tax suggestion on the grounds that it might be inequitable to families with large numbers of children. Buchanan's argument would seem to indicate that disproportionate costs on large families would seem to be a *desirable* result on grounds of *efficiency*.

In the context of the Coase theorem, the question of who takes the initiative certainly depends on the initial structure of rights. Let us accept without question the property right alternative that Buchanan poses in his model: either parents *do not* have the rights to produce children unless they are prepared to pay the full costs, or they *do* possess such rights. How does this reasoning apply to the problem that is central to my own analysis and to the real world? Under present American practice parents fall into *both* of the property rights categories. Parents who use public schools are nearer the category of those who can produce children without paying the full costs. Those parents who use parochial schools, in contrast, are nearer to the other category of those who do not have these rights. No doubt much of the problem associated with the First Amendment and discussed in my essay is that of *defining* the relevant property rights; this is the concern of the jurists and of what Buchanan calls the "protective" (as distinct from the "productive") state. Until such property rights are finally and clearly defined, and in the absence of the "family control" subsidies he describes, I have a lurking and disturbing thought when applying Buchanan's model: the dominant secular majority *might be actively desiring* the present asymmetrical structure of rights—because this will eventually reduce the proportion of parochial to secular individuals in the population to a lower level than would otherwise occur. If this is really the case, then it is legitimate to ask whether *it* squares with the ideals of liberty that were attempted in the original American Constitution, and specially with that part of it that is contained in the First Amendment. Conversely, if user taxes were introduced these would encourage not only economic efficiency, as Buchanan shows, but also economic equity (or justice).

The other extreme considered in Buchanan's model is the case where education is entirely a private good (i.e., there are no public or external benefits) but where *for some reason* the community finances its schooling through general taxation levied on the whole community membership. Because such a form of finance will modify incentives for the creation of children, Buchanan supports my recommended departure from it in favor of a user tax—but mainly for this additional reason. Again much depends on personal judgment. If Buchanan, like Friedman, believes that external benefits are zero at the margin, the logic of user tax pricing supported by this additional reasoning seems unanswerable. One is left, however, with the question of why Buchanan postulated a world where education is financed through the public purse despite the fact that it yields private benefits exclusively. What is the particular reason for such a system, even in imagination? Redistribution in favor of poor families might be one argument. It is not a very persuasive one, however, since other more efficient means of achieving it are available. And if redistribution *were* the main argument, it would not lead to a case for *universal* free education, but only to free education for those who required positive assistance. A second and more plausible argument has been suggested by me several times already. It is that community finance of education is needed to offset a capital market imperfection. In other words, a system of public finance of education might be efficient in helping persons to draw upon their lifetime incomes in a way that would not be possible otherwise. If *this* is the case, however, I come back to the point that government intervention is primarily called for on financial, not educational, grounds. Such financial facilities could take the form of universal loans or 'vouchers' spendable at parochial as well as at other schools. This arrangement would not infringe on the First Amendment; yet parochial schools would be better off than they are now.

Strategies for Preserving Educational Freedom

Donald A. Erickson

While many facets of West's paper warrant discussion, the available space permits me to focus only on what are, from my viewpoint, the three most important considerations: (1) the timeliness of the paper, (2) some implications of the light it throws on the Supreme Court's doctrine concerning "parochiaid," and (3) the promise inherent in user charges in public schools, proposed by West as a way of preserving private educational options.

Timeliness

Factors now at work, including an unprecedented combination of inflation and recession, could obliterate most nonpublic schools—at a time, ironically, when there is probably greater manifest need than ever for a broad range of educational alternatives, and when there is evidence that most Americans favor state assistance to keep nonpublic schools alive.[1]

If the nation's nonpublic schools are abandoned, numerous cities may be unable, as West observes, to pump enough money through their overloaded taxation conduits to accommodate the additional students in public schools without compromising instructional quality. Even when adequate funds are available, a mixed system of publicly and privately funded schools seems more likely than an exclusively public system to respond to the heterogeneous demands of students and their families and to experiment with new procedures.[2] There has been little tendency in tax-supported schools to allocate varying amounts of money to the instruction of youngsters who need different quantities and types of tutelage, and the programs purchased by the money have been strikingly standardized.[3] Since nonpublic schools are established specifically to provide what public schools are perceived as not providing, and since they are patronized by choice, one would expect them to be more closely attuned than most public schools to varying client needs. Dissatisfied patrons are not only free to go elsewhere, but (unlike their public school confrères) when they leave, they take their money along. Nonpublic schools have special reasons for being responsive.

In all likelihood, nonpublic schools as a whole experiment no more than public schools as a whole, but at several critical junctures the explorations

---

Prepared for the Center for Independent Education, December 30, 1974.

124

of a few private trailblazers have had an enormous impact.[4] One of the more recent examples is the vastly disproportionate influence of five or six independent schools in the creation of Advanced Placement programs and new curricula in mathematics and the physical sciences.[5]

But the most compelling reasons for educational options are ethical and humanitarian. Inestimable misery has resulted from the imposition of majoritarian ideologies and life-styles in schools.[a] Children from disliked minorities repeatedly have been harassed through the powerful systems of peer influence that schools generate, and at times by teachers, administrators, and school boards. Anguished parents have stood by, often helplessly, while their children have been tormented and even alienated from their homes and communities. The oppressed minorities have included gentle Amish, aggressive Jehovah's Witnesses, militant atheists, pacifists in wartime, impassive American Indians, Greek-Americans trying to maintain traditions extending back to Socrates, Catholics in predominantly Protestant schools, Jews in predominantly Christian schools, black children in newly integrated Southern schools, poor children in middle-class schools, and many more.[6] Nonpublic schools have provided some members of such groups with settings hospitable to their values and life-styles, but disturbing questions can be raised about a framework of public policy that denies this avenue of escape to others.

Within the current legal structure, this avenue of escape is not only limited (since many cannot afford it) but critically jeopardized. It encountered one major crisis during 1965-1966, with a decline in the demand for traditional parochial schooling. The Catholic schools experienced a precipitous enrollment decline and a cascade of fiscal emergencies, largely because, it appears, the advent of ecumenicity in the Catholic church was destroying the old reasons for parochial schooling.[7] The cloistered boarding schools were hard hit by a passion among youth for involvement in social issues.[8] Military schools withered in the wake of the hated Vietnam war. Many sexually segregated schools were forced to choose between becoming coeducational and going out of business.

At the same time, new educational preferences were emerging; but schools created in response seldom attracted wealthy clients or church subvention, and thus they were fiscally vulnerable. Witness the private free schools, which blossomed briefly during the late 1960s and early 1970s.[9] While there is disagreement concerning the precise mortality rate among

[a] In effect, our current arrangements for education permit local majorities, functioning by means of school boards, to impose their favorite values and patterns of behavior upon the local public schools (within very minimal constitutional restrictions), regardless of the feelings and convictions of minorities who must patronize those schools. But the most powerful aspect of this imposition is largely unintentional, and perhaps largely unavoidable, consisting of the social sanctions that students impose on their peers to force them to behave according to the local norms.

private free schools, it is obviously very high, and observers who follow the movement closely think it has lost much ground.[10] Many free-school failures seem largely attributable to the fact that, since neither rich clients nor religious grants are available, such schools typically operate on a shoestring, relying on extraordinary contributed services from a few people, who soon are debilitated physically and financially.[11]

Nonpublic schools with access to wealthy clients (seldom catering exclusively to the wealthy, however), having tightened their financial belts and adapted to numerous shifting preferences, are maintaining a relatively steady state at present.[12] Religiously affiliated schools not seriously affected by ecumenicity have held their own and in some cases experienced significant growth, thanks to major religious subsidies in most cases.[13] But since more than 75 percent of all nonpublic schools are Catholic, the Catholic school losses, combined with other losses discussed earlier, produced a sobering net decline for nonpublic education as a whole. Between 1965 and 1966 and between 1970 and 1971, the estimated total national enrollment dropped by 12.3 percent.[14] The proportion of the nation's student population attending nonpublic schools decreased from an all-time high of 13.6 percent in 1959-1960 to 11.0 percent in 1970-1971.[15] By all indications, there has been further absolute and relative deterioration since 1970-1971.

The current situation is a recapitulation of the history of nonpublic schools in the United States. Few nonpublic schools survived for long in the past or are surviving for long at present without access either to monied clients or to extensive help from religious institutions. The reasons are not difficult to discover. Our society imposes financial penalties, artificial "threshold costs," on patrons of nonpublic schools. Parents who move their child from a public school costing (through taxation) $1,000 per pupil annually to a nonpublic school costing $1,300 per pupil annually must pay, not the difference of $300, but the entire $1,300, unless some aid is available, for the parents cannot transfer, along with their child, the child's share of tax money for education. As a consequence of being required to "pay twice," the unsubsidized patron of the nonpublic school experiences an approximately double impact when costs rise.[b] If public school taxation increases to the maximum that families of a given income level can afford, nonpublic schools lacking subvention will have been priced out of reach of these families.

Within the past few months, a second crisis has struck the nation's nonpublic schools, though the consequences are not yet evident. This crisis

---

[b] Either the nonpublic school will spend approximately as much additional money as the public schools are spending, or it will appear to fall behind in quality. In either case, the client will "pay," and as costs continue to rise, will have increasing reason to reconsider the decision to patronize a nonpublic school.

has been produced by simultaneous inflation and recession, which are seriously eroding the purchasing power of most families. In such a context, educational costs cannot continue spiraling at anything like the recent rate (5 times the rate of inflation, according to a study cited by West) without soon destroying most nonpublic schools. Times like these are particularly deadly for schools not underwritten by religious institutions or patronized by the affluent. In addition, the proportion of nonpublic schools with access to religious subsidies seems likely to decline much further as ecumenicity devastates traditional motivations for parochial schooling in group after group.[16]

It is a good time to consider, as West has done, the strategies for preserving our educational freedom.

The "Hands-off" Doctrine

As West observes, a consistent taboo on governmental policies that reduce the costs of religious endeavors could lead to ridiculous extremes:

Suppose the government made large purchases of a certain kind of timber for use in a new public housing program. Suppose that the sawing of the timber created a considerable by-product of sawdust, and of the quality which happens to be exactly right for burning incense in churches. Incense was previously a high cost factor in religion, but now its cost was dramatically reduced. Such a government housing project would presumably not be struck down as an aid to religion even though it has the consequence of advancing religion.

More important, perhaps, West's analysis of the unavoidable entanglement of the costs of various goods and services suggests to me (in a slight departure from West's emphasis) that recent Supreme Court decisions have created a grossly inequitable institutionalized bias.

At one time, the Supreme Court began to apply a balancing test when assessing the constitutionality of state infringements on religious liberty.[17] The seriousness of a given infringement was weighed against the urgency of the state's objectives. The state was not permitted to trammel religious liberty for the sake of unimportant governmental purposes, and even urgent state interests could not be permitted to transgress against religious freedom if alternative policies were available to achieve the urgent state objectives without thus transgressing. It was not enough for government to maintain separation from churches, ignoring religion as much as possible. Active efforts were required to preserve neutrality.

In the landmark "parochiaid" case of *Lemon v. Kurtzman,* the Supreme Court said nothing about these standards of religious neutrality.[18] State actions (such as the purchase of secular educational services from church-related schools) that had the effect of *reducing* the costs of religious activities (such as religious indoctrination in church-related schools) were forbidden. Since the Court has not forbidden state actions that *increase* the costs of religious activities, one major effect of the *Lemon* decision, I fear, is to institutionalize hostility toward religion. The states have been allocating larger and larger proportions of family incomes to public education (through taxation) while simultaneously requiring patrons of nonpublic schools to "pay twice." As a result of this twin policy, nonpublic schools are steadily being priced out of the market. Yet, the Supreme Court has ruled, the states may not take the compensatory step of reducing these religious costs by such means as purchasing secular educational services from parochial schools or providing tax credits or deductions to the patrons. The states are not even required to finance public schools in ways (assuming they can be found) that do not gradually price nonpublic schools into oblivion.[c] If the states were consistently "blind" toward religious consequences, the positive and negative effects on religion of various public policies would tend to balance each other out; but when the states are blind toward the negative effects and forbidden to be blind toward, or "guilty" of, the positive effects, the system is inequitable.

These recently buttressed inequities further underline the timeliness of West's presentation, and especially his discussion of methods of public school funding that would reduce or eliminate the financial handicaps now imposed on nonpublic schools. Some scholars (this writer among them) have concluded that the Supreme Court's current stance concerning the use of public funds in church-related schools reflects not so much the systematic extension of jurisprudential guidelines as a basic aversion to this use of funds per se, partly because the Court is convinced that an unavoidable result would be political strife along religious lines.[19] The Court apparently has not considered the quite plausible alternative—that here, as apparently in the Netherlands, giving church-related schools a fair chance to survive could *reduce* interdenominational bitterness.[20] At any rate, the Court might well react, when confronted with analyses (such as West's) that destroy the doctrinal basis of recent rulings, not by altering its position, but by creating new doctrines to bolster the present posture. Realistically, the future of private educational alternatives may depend on radical changes in the structure of school finance—changes that remove the handicaps now destroying nonpublic schools, including many schools now struggling to be born, without invoking the bogey of "aid" to church-related schools.

---

[c] In fairness it must be pointed out that, so far as I am aware, this precise issue has never been presented squarely to the Court. So far as the nature of the existing system of school finance is concerned, however, the results are the same as if the issue had been presented and decided.

Positive Pricing

West suggests a framework of public policy within which all or some of the costs of public schooling would fall exclusively on citizens who send their children to public schools. Taxation mechanisms could be used as a loan system, to let people pay for public pedagogical services on the basis of life-long incomes, rather than on incomes during the relatively few years when their children are in school. West observes essentially (if I may run some risk of oversimplification) that, since most people have school-age children at some point, the new approach would not produce radically different fiscal results, as compared with current arrangements, except that nonpublic school patrons would be relieved of the financial handicaps now imposed upon them. The Supreme Court would have to go to ridiculous lengths to view these people (and others exempt from at least a proportion of public school taxes) as recipients of "public aid," and no political warfare should be triggered along sectarian frontiers.

West deals remarkably well with the initial shocked objections that his ideas seem certain to produce. He notes, for example, that numerous equalization arrangements could be introduced to assist the poor who, despite the alleged merits of current school finance, pay for the "free" education of their offspring through taxes that draw considerably larger percentages of their income than the rich are required to contribute. He also points out that children would continue to be protected by compulsory attendance laws.

In the light of West's analysis and my reading of recent events, I lean to the view that positive pricing, along the lines he lays out, is the most promising approach available at present for preserving and perhaps expanding our educational liberties.[21] But the American citizenry has shown little readiness thus far to support radical reform in education, organized teachers and administrators have repeatedly demonstrated the power to block developments that threaten their vested interests, and West's ideas are not yet specific enough to be put into operation. The road ahead will be rough, at best. We had better produce a map, a master plan, a strategy, a model statute, before proceeding too far. To cite an analogy, we are approximately at the stage where advocates of education vouchers found themselves soon after Friedman's celebrated 1955 essay.[22] To rush into the legislatures in 1955 could have been disastrous, an efficient way of aborting a powerful concept.

Many important questions must now be examined systematically. To mention just a few: Of the various forms a positive pricing framework might take, what models seem most promising, and what are their strengths and weaknesses? How can the negative potential of each be minimized or avoided? How can we best capitalize on the potential strengths? Should all public school costs, or only a portion of them, be borne exclusively by the users? If a major proportion of public school funds is to be so derived, and if these funds are to be derived from the lifetime incomes of the users, how shall we deal with people who become identifiable as users only late in life (because they have children later than usual)? Should competitive conditions for public schools be built into the system? What is the best way (in the light of administrative, fiscal, political, and constitutional considerations) of moving from current arrangements to the new financing scheme? (Is it better to terminate public education altogether and then begin *de novo* two months later, or should one "phase into" the positive pricing gradually, perhaps beginning with a policy requiring the users of public schooling to shoulder the entire burden of *future* cost increases?) What taxation mechanism or government-guaranteed loan system, if any, can be made available constitutionally to patrons of religiously affiliated schools? What is the best way of giving the rich and the poor access to reasonably equal educational opportunities? How shall we deal with issues of racial segregation? With unscrupulous purveyors of educational services? With school officials who deprive students of their civil rights? How can the rights of children best be protected against those few parents who shirk their responsibilities? How can the plan be made as palatable as possible to the major lobbies that might otherwise destroy it in the legislatures? How can we minimize the chances that a new bureaucratic leviathan will capture and debauch the proposed arrangements? What self-correcting devices should be created to revise and improve the system as evidence concerning its consequences emerges?

To answer these questions hurriedly would be to shoot from the hip, at best. I think we need some functional equivalent of the intensive, interdisciplinary study of education vouchers conducted by several groups of scholars (perhaps most notably by Christopher Jencks and his colleagues at the Center for the Study of Public Policy). Hopefully, the current collection of comments on West's analysis will provide the necessary springboard for the work that remains to be done.

Notes

1. The need for a great deal more diverse response to differential student needs and interests was the topic of a presidential address at the 1972 meeting of the American Educational Research Association. See Robert Glaser, "Individuals and Learnings: The New Aptitudes," *Educational Researcher,* 1(June 1972): 5-13. Considerable scholarly attention has been given to this need since it became evident that the massive

"Coleman study" was seriously handicapped in its search for effective school practices by the lack of diversity in the practices of his national sample of schools. See Eric A. Hanuschek and John F. Kain, "On the Value of *Equality of Educational Opportunity* as a Guide to Public Policy," in Frederick Mosteller and Daniel P. Moynihan, eds., *On Equality of Educational Opportunity* (New York: Random House, 1972), pp. 116-145. Many studies of schooling among various ethnic groups have lamented the fact that little adaptation to the cultures of such groups can be found in the schools. The recent National Study of American Indian Education is a prominent example. See Estelle Fuchs and Robert J. Havighurst, *To Live on This Earth* (New York: Doubleday & Company, 1972). The demand for educational diversity is a major explanation for the private "free schools" and the public "alternative schools." See Allen Graubard, *Free the Children: Radical Reform and the Free School Movement* (New York: Pantheon Books, 1972); and Mario D. Fantini, *Public Schools of Choice* (New York: Random House, 1971). The latest annual Gallup poll on attitudes toward public education revealed that a majority of respondents favored a constitutional amendment to permit state aid to parochial schools. See George H. Gallup, "Sixth Annual Gallup Poll of Public Attitudes toward Education," *Phi Delta Kappan* 61(September, 1974): 25.

2. Mark V. Pauly, "Mixed Public and Private Financing of Education: Efficiency and Feasibility," *American Economic Review,* 57(March 1967): 120-130.

3. Glaser, "Individuals and Learning"; Hanuschek and Kain, "On the Value"; Fuchs and Havighurst, *To Live on This Earth.*

4. Donald A. Erickson, "The Trailblazer in an Age of R&D," *School Review,* 81(February 1973): 155-174.

5. Roy A. Larmee, "The Relationship between Certain National Movements in Education and Selected Independent Secondary Schools" (Ph.D. dissertation, University of Chicago, 1962); and his "National Movements and Independent Schools," in Roald F. Campbell and Robert A. Bunnell, eds., *Nationalizing Influences on Secondary Education* (Chicago: Midwest Administration Center, University of Chicago, 1963), pp. 105-118.

6. Since the literature on this topic is so voluminous, the following examples must suffice: Donald A. Erickson, "The 'Plain People' and American Democracy," *Commentary,* 45(January 1968): 36-44; David R. Manwaring, *Render Unto Caesar: The Flag-Salute Controversy* (Chicago: University of Chicago Press, 1962); Rosalie H. Wax, "The Warrior Dropouts," *Transaction,* 4(May 1967): 40-46; Andrew Thomas Kopan, "Education and Greek Immigrants in Chicago, 1892-1973: A Study in Ethnic Survival" (Ph.D. dissertation, University of Chicago, 1974); Leo Pfeffer,

Church, State and Freedom, rev. ed. (Boston: Beacon Press, 1967), Chapter 9; August B. Hollingshead, *Elmtown's Youth: The Impact of Social Classes on Adolescents* (New York: John Wiley & Sons, 1949).

7. For the most comprehensive analysis of factors behind the Catholic school enrollment decline, to my knowledge, see John D. Donovan, Donald A. Erickson, and George F. Madaus, *The Social and Religious Sources of the Crisis in Catholic Schools,* Vol. 2 of *Issues of Aid to Nonpublic Schools,* A Report to the President's Commission on School Finance (Washington, D.C.: the Commission, 1971).

8. Information concerning the boarding, military, and single-sex independent schools has been drawn mostly from discussions with officials of the National Association of Independent Schools in Boston.

9. Graubard, *Free the Children;* Bruce S. Cooper, *Free and Freedom Schools: A National Survey of Alternative Programs,* A Report to the President's Commission of School Finance (Washington: the Commission, 1972).

10. This statement is based on my own observations, plus those of my colleague, Bruce Cooper (author of *Free and Freedom Schools*), plus queries directed by telephone during the last weeks of 1974 to free-school leaders in several areas of the nation by Cooper, in my behalf. His assistance in this regard is gratefully acknowledged.

11. Graubard, *Free the Children*; Cooper, *Free and Freedom Schools* and "Organizational Survival: A Comparative Case Study of Seven American 'Free Schools'" (Ph.D. dissertation, University of Chicago, 1974).

12. Based on discussions with leaders of the National Association of Independent Schools, Boston, during the late months of 1974.

13. Officials of the Lutheran Church—Missouri Synod, in St. Louis—report that enrollment totals in affiliated elementary schools are down 4.3 percent (as of 1973-1974) from the totals in 1965-1966. Officials of the National Union of Christian Schools in Grand Rapids, Michigan, report that NUSC schools (associated with the Christian Reformed Church) gained 1.7 percent in total enrollment between 1965-1966 and 1973-1974. Officials of the American Lutheran Church report a 46.4 percent growth in total enrollment in the schools (less than 170 in number) associated with ALC. Officials of the National Association of Christian Schools (Wheaton, Illinois) report a 66.1 percent growth in enrollment in member schools between 1965-1966 and 1973-1974. Officials of the General Conference of Seventh-Day Adventists (Washington, D.C.) report a 15.9 percent enrollment increase in elementary schools in the U.S. and a 14.2 percent enrollment increase in secondary schools in the U.S. between 1965-1966 and 1973-1974. Officials of the Wisconsin Evangelical Lutheran Synod report a

6.8 percent increase in elementary schools and a 29.1 percent increase in secondary schools between 1965-1966 and 1973-1974. Officials of the National Association of Episcopal Schools (Washington, D.C.) estimate that Episcopal schools gained around 60 percent in enrollment between 1965-1966 and 1973-1974. Officials of the National Society for Hebrew Day Schools report that their member schools experienced extremely rapid "spurt" growth for several years after 1965-1966, but are now in a period of "slow, steady growth." Virtually all officials contacted in this regard reported that the rate of enrollment gains had considerably declined during the past year or so.

14. Based on a comparison of data in the following sources: Otto F. Krauschaar, *American Nonpublic Schools: Patterns of Diversity* (Baltimore: Johns Hopkins Press, 1972), p. 14; U.S. Office of Education, *Statistics of Nonpublic Elementary and Secondary Schools, 1970-71* (DHEW Publication No. OE 74-11420).

15. Ibid.

16. Over a long period of time in the United States, religious groups originally very "sectarian" and exclusive in orientation have "joined the denominational fold," becoming more and more ecumenical. Some writers have traced this trend to basic social forces in the United States. One sees little reason why these processes will not continue. See H. Richard Neibuhr, *The Social Sources of Denominationalism* (New York: Henry Holt, 1929); Will Herberg, *Protestant, Catholic, Jew,* rev. ed. (Garden City, N.Y.: Anchor Books, 1960).

17. The development of the balancing test and numerous court cases involving it are discussed at length in the following articles: Marc Galanter, "Religious Freedoms in the United States: A Turning Point?" *Wisconsin Law Review* 1966(Spring, 1966): 217-296; Donald A. Giannella, "Religious Liberty, Nonestablishment, and Doctrinal Development; Part I: The Religious Liberty Guarantee," *Harvard Law Review* 80(May 1967): 1381-1431.

18. *Lemon v. Kurtzman,* 403 U.S. 602 (1971).

19. Giannella comments, for example: "In the *Allen* case in 1967, the Court went over the verge and sanctioned the free loan of textbooks. In *Lemon* the Court sought to scramble back, reaching out for any support it could find on the constitutional landscape. The nearest at hand was the 'excessive entanglement' notion recently enunciated in the *Walz* case. . . . Although the reasoning of the Court in these cases offers little guidance, one may detect an underlying disposition to restrict assistance [to church-related schools] at the elementary and secondary levels." Donald A. Giannella, "Lemon and Tilton: The Bitter and the Sweet of Church-State Entanglement," in Philip B. Kurland, ed., *Supreme Court Review, 1971* (Chicago: University of Chicago Press, 1972), p. 148. Agree-

ing with Giannella concerning the basic disposition of the Supreme Court toward any significant transfer of money from public coffers to church-related schools, Morgan has a different explanation of the origins of the "excessive entanglement" doctine: "Far from being a branch clutched in panic, *Walz* appears a carefully planted post which was to allow the Court to negotiate the 'slippery slope' of aid to church schools by disallowing any program which brought government into direct contact with church schools. . . ." Richard E. Morgan, "The Establishment Clause and Sectarian Schools: A Final Installment?" in Kurland, *Supreme Court Review, 1972,* p. 74. Both Morgan and Giannella stress the Court's fear of interdenominational strife, though Giannella does not view that fear as the Court's most basic motive. But in reading the landmark "parochiaid" cases of 1971 and 1973, one encounters many paragraphs of discussion devoted to the issue of political strife along religious lines.

20. It is the contention of an eminent Dutch sociologist that the decision to provide equal tax support to nonsectarian and sectarian schools in the Netherlands did much to defuse the religious strife that had been rampant for decades. Unfortunately, his paper has not yet been widely circulated, and a widespread impression that religious devisiveness in the Netherlands was sparked by this decision on funding continues to be manifest in the United States. See C.E. Vervoort, "Social Consequences of Financial Parity of Public and Private Education, the Dutch Case," in Donald A. Erickson and George F. Madaus, *Economic and Social Issues of Educational Pluralism,* Vol. 1 of Erickson and Madaus, *Issues of Aid to Nonpublic Schools,* A Report to the President's Commission on School Finance (Washington, D.C.: the Commission, 1972), pp. III:A:1-III:A:55.

21. I continue to see important potential in voucher experiments and in a considerable extension of the principles embodied in public "alternative schools." My article discussing the latter approach is scheduled to appear in the January-February 1975 issue of *Religious Education.*

22. Milton Friedman, "The Role of Government in Education," in Robert A. Solo, ed., *Economics and the Public Interest* (New Brunswick, N.J.: Rutgers University Press, 1955), pp. 123-153.

Response to Erickson: The Practical Barriers

E.G. West

Those who share Erickson's belief that inestimable misery has resulted from the imposition of majoritarian ideologies on children from disliked minorities, will see another dimension to the problem of equity in education. If we are concerned with educational welfare in its widest setting, we must assess it as involving more than monetary considerations. Thus while Coons and Sugarman are interested in district power equalizing, their system might have little defense against the psychological or welfare inequalities mentioned by Erickson. The only way to meet this problem, according to Erickson, is to allow maximum free choice for families. This would seem to augment my reasoning in the response to Coons, that the lack of "fair shares" expresses itself most seriously in the unfair share of choices available. Yet it would seem that the Supreme Court in the *Nyquist* case would need no persuasion on this issue, for indeed the Court argued that pluralism was a desirable social target that is welcome in the twentieth century. We are still left, therefore, with the main problem of resolving the question of barriers to free choice that the First Amendment seems to contain on present judicial interpretation.

There are two aspects to any discussion on this matter. First, the participants may concentrate on previous errors of judgment within the Supreme Court. Second, they may focus on solutions that are possible *despite* "erroneous" judicial interpretation. The first approach is necessary and useful, but it is not likely to get short-term results. I support Erickson's criticisms of the Court that its recent decisions have revealed an inequitable institutionalized bias. Indeed I suppose I was making the same kind of point when I concluded my response to Sugarman with the question of why the Court is so sensitive to positive acts of government in aiding parochial schools but less sensitive when governments have in the past been imposing injuries on the same schools. If the Court must monitor legislation for religious intent, should it not be equally vigilant for the Free Exercise clause as well as for the Establishment clause?

Erickson supports the logic of my argument for the return of positive pricing to education. He is concerned, however, with some practical problems in implementation. I believe that some of, but not all, these will prove to be challenging. The most important obstacle that Erickson indicates is the power of organized teachers and administrators to "block developments that threaten their vested interests." Administrators, teachers, supervisors, and custodians are in effect members of a huge

135

bureaucracy—in the widest sense of that term. One of the important findings of the new discipline called "the economics of politics" is that producer interests will tend to dominate consumer interests in political activity. The producer interests in this case are represented by the huge "army of employees" in the educational bureaucracy. These governmental employees have political voting rights, and these are normally used to favor increases and to oppose reductions in budgeted outlay. Moreover, the producer rents that they enjoy stem from the overall monopoly position that is a feature of the present public school system. Another new discipline, "the economics of bureaucracy," finds that "consumer's surplus" benefit is much better squeezed to the benefit of the suppliers when the latter constituted a one monolithic monopoly.[1] Since the return to positive pricing is a threat to monopoly structure, one must predict and anticipate opposition to my proposal for this reason alone.

Yet the more one is impressed by this obstacle, the greater the potential scope for cost reductions in education. With more competition the ability of suppliers to extract consumers' surpluses from the voters will be reduced, excessive bureaucratic expenditure will fall, and innovations will more likely be introduced. Insofar as it is the poorest sections of society that are locked into the public school system, it is they who stand to gain the biggest increase in education per tax dollar contributed. This point has important bearing on the concern for equity that has been shown by Coons and Sugarman, a concern *they* hope to meet by a reshuffling (and perhaps strengthening) of the existing bureaucratic structure rather than by a weakening of it.

Suppose the members of the giant bureaucracy in education have the dominant influence in decision making. We would then start from a position of almost total intransigence at the legislative level. The only hope that remains for those who wish to reestablish parental choice, competition, and diversity is that the Supreme Court will eventually yield to the kind of joint supply arguments I have been making and admit that previous judicial decision has been in error. A new and vigorous reinterpretation of the First Amendment might then emerge that would threaten the monopoly structure of the public schooling, to the benefit not only of parochial users but of others as well. Such thoughts are obviously very optimistic. But we need not interpret the situation in this manner. It is not inevitable that bureaucratic votes are the dominant ones. General public opinion can still be a force in itself. It is true that empirical evidence shows that the proportion of government employees (e.g. teachers and administrators) who vote is significantly higher than the proportion of nongovernment employees. This need not always be the case in education, especially if the public imagination is captured by the sort of new and active discussion that is being generated in this book. Parents have votes too; and they are a sizable and potentially dominant interest group. Moreover government employees are parents. Significantly, the New York legislation that attempted to aid parochial schools was *not* defeated by the administration, the teachers, and other employees of the education bureau; the legislation was defeated by the Supreme Court. In other words, the voters, as consumers of education, seem to have come so far with their well-articulated preferences for modest aid for private schools. Conjectures about bureaucratic opposition, therefore, may be less relevant. We must avoid attempting to cross bridges we have not yet encountered.

With respect to Erickson's questions concerning other practical difficulties, I have dealt with several of them already in my responses to other writers. He asks, for instance, how we can deal with people who become users of public schools only late in life because they have children later than usual. My answer is contained in my discussion of income-contingent loan schemes in my response to Sugarman. On the question of the best way of moving from current arrangements to the new financing scheme, I believe I have already indicated that the practical method is to impose marginal user fees in the future so as to confine them to cost increases. It so happens that such increases will bring financial relief to the parochial schools in roughly the same magnitude as the relief that was attempted in the New York legislation. This method, therefore, would seem to be the most politically feasible. Of course once prices are charged, however small, the myth of "free education" will begin to dissolve. This might well pave the way for further switching to direct, and away from indirect, payment. The initial move, incidentally, will begin to meet Erickson's question: Should competitive conditions for public schools be built into the system? As parents withdraw their child from one school and enroll her/him in another, they will now transfer *some* educational finance automatically. This alone will bring increased respect for parents' wishes and ensure *some* element of competition. Erickson's question about how we shall deal with unscrupulous purveyors of educational services is also, to a large extent, answered by increased competition. In the long run, when parents have had more experience with choice, the more inefficient suppliers of educational services are not likely to survive. Indeed it is agreed by many that it is in the present, largely protected, educational system that inefficient suppliers are more likely to prevail. The question of how the rights of children can best be protected against the few parents who are irresponsible applies equally to the present system. I do not see that the adoption of my proposal will make it any more likely that the irresponsible parent will be more neglectful. The laws on compulsory education will still remain, and these are the main protection that children have at present against irresponsible parents.

Finally, I think Erickson is rather too cautious about the timing of new schemes. I don't agree with him that it would have been disastrous to legislate shortly after Friedman's 1955 essay. I do not believe that the voucher schemes such as the one being tried at Alum Rock have benefited from such a long wait. Meanwhile discussion has been hindered by the absence of real facts concerning the way such schemes could operate. We have consequently suffered twenty years of unsatisfactory a priori debate.

Argument has been impeded by repeated references to hypothetical dangers and unsubstantiated fears. The best time to introduce educational innovation no doubt is when the circumstances are fit. The immediate present is one such time, for taxpayers are increasingly reluctant to finance school bond issues and pay increased property taxes to finance the growing expenses of education. Switching marginally to a tax upon parents could be modest in scale—say $1 per week for the first child, $.50 for the second, $.25 for the third. Such sums are of the magnitude necessary to help significantly to meet annual cost increases. The fees in the subsequent year would of course rise again. While modest in scale initially, the change would be a fairly dramatic one conceptually and symbolically; but this one *could* succeed judicially, economically, and politically.

Note

1. W.A. Niskanen, *Bureaucracy and Representative Government,* Aldine-Atherton, New York, 1971.

Universal Choice as the Key Issue

James D. Koerner

West's article is by far the most penetrating of the theoretical arguments that have been made for salvaging the parochial schools with public money. I put it this way so as not to cloud the central issue. No matter how ingenious the devices or the labels that can be invented by friends of the parochial schools, of whom I count myself one, for the financial relief of thse institutions, any such help is going to continue to be seen as public assistance to private institutions. The adoption of West's principal scheme might help us toward other goals, such as educational pluralism, but these would be secondary effects. The main effect would be to free Catholic parents from having to pay twice for the schooling of their children and to free non-Catholic parents who like Catholic schools from having to do the same thing.

I leave it to others to comment on the intricate technical aspects of the argument, economic and legal, and confine myself to its educational implications. But perhaps I can be permitted in passing to record my own bias on the constitutional question. The courts have seemed to me for many years overly rigid in their interpretation of the religious clauses of the First Amendment. Most of what goes on in parochial schools—certainly in these days after Vatican II and the astonishing liberalization, for better or worse, of Catholic doctrine and practice—is conventional schooling, not religious education or indoctrination.

It is therefore difficult to see that letting parochial schools close would be in the public interest. (Catholic colleges are a different question. Some of them are in an even worse squeeze than parochial schools, having to compete for students with other private colleges as well as with low-cost public institutions. And some of them, I regret to say, like some sectarian private colleges, are demonstrating that established institutions will do anything at all to survive.) There seems to this non-Catholic observer every justification for the state to support parochial schools, however it can be done to satisfy the Constitution, in recognition of their function in the ordinary education of future citizens.

Some readers are apt to assume that the principal aim of West's paper has to do with widening the range of choice for students and parents, introducing competition among schools, and fostering a free market in primary and secondary education. That is not his immediate aim, but his program might well move us toward these desirable goals. Although West does not try to deal with the purely educational ramifications of his paper, it

139

might be useful for us to speculate about them. What are the implications for the kind and quality of education offered in public and private schools if West's pure model were adopted? What if one of the modified proposals were adopted, such as financing only the increase in school costs over some base period through a user tax? Unfortunately, we have little experience with free-market or modified-free-market education to be guided by, especially in this century. So speculation it will have to be.

Suppose we ask the basic question in a slightly different way: how many parents are content enough with the education offered in the public schools that they would be unlikely to switch to a private school offering a different kind of education if they had the opportunity? For that matter, how many would switch to a different public school if the program were really different and they had the option? To my knowledge, no one has ever polled a national, regional, or statewide sample of parents on such a question; neither has the vast majority of individual school districts. What experiments there have been in permitting parents to choose among public schools have been so few—and those few hedged with so many restrictions—that conclusions are risky, although trends are discernible. Still, we at best can see through the glass, darkly.

Other evidence, however, suggests that parental dissatisfaction is indeed widespread. In the inner-city schools anywhere in the country, "parental dissatisfaction" is obviously an inadequate phrase—nobody, except perhaps selected administrators, is happy with these schools. In rural areas and smaller towns, and in especially depressed areas like Appalachia, views are more mixed, although parents may be less dissatisfied than are outside observers who tell them they should be too.

It seems safe to say that the level of expressed dissatisfaction in the suburbs is rarely low but rarely high. Individual voices crying alarm are always heard, as a random reading of any suburban newspaper will reveal, but a certain forbearance tempers educational debate in suburbia except on those occasions when parental frustration reaches a flash point over one issue or another. But the absence of boisterous debate signifies neither apathy nor satisfaction. Many parents simply have limited time and appetite for fighting a monolithic public education establishment; many also fear reprisals against their own children. Moreover, they have never had a chance to exercise choice in programs or schools and so have never given a public indication of how they would respond to such an opportunity.

What we can say with certainty is that the educational wars of the last twenty years are an eloquent demonstration of the fact that a very large, if undetermined, percentage of American parents want a different education for their children from the one offered (that is to say, required) in their public schools. The war over reading, for example, or over the "new curricula," or the training and competence of teachers, or the loss of geography in the miasma of social studies, or the philosophy of "life adjustment,'' ''consumer education,'' ''career education'' or a dozen other panaceas, or simply over the level of literacy attained in basic subjects by those who complete twelve years of schooling—all these tormented controversies surely tell us something about the unhappiness of parents with public schools. When parents become unhappy enough, they opt out of the system altogether if they can afford it. Most cannot afford it and so remain captives of their own tax-supported educational system.

Five years ago the nation had an opportunity to test the proposition that many parents, given half a chance, would pick a different program or a different school from the one their children were in, and would do so not on geographical, racial, or social grounds but on educational grounds. The Office of Economic Opportunity invited applications from, and made grants to, school districts wanting to examine the feasibility of integrating a ''regulated compensatory voucher plan'' into their school systems. Only six school systems in the country took up OEO's offer: Gary (Indiana), Seattle, San Francisco, New Rochelle, Rochester, and Alum Rock Union Elementary (San José). And only one of the six, Alum Rock, having completed the feasibility study, sought a planning and later an implementation grant. The other five decided that the politics of even a severely restricted voucher plan were too hot to handle. Minority groups saw the whole idea as a racist plot; teachers' unions saw it as a threat to their jobs; and state legislatures were not at all amenable to passing enabling legislation that would allow nonpublic schools to take part in the experiment.

Hence Alum Rock is the only voucher experiment to be conducted to date, and it is still far from completed. In fact, it operates under so many constraints that it is less an experiment in vouchers than in simply providing students with enrichment and some parents with a choice in schools and programs. Parochial schools are barred from the project, as have been, until very recently, private nonreligious schools. After prolonged and heated debate, the California legislature recently passed enabling legislation that will permit Alum Rock to contract with private, nonreligious organizations to operate schools as a part of the voucher system.

In spite of the heavy ''regulation'' of the Alum Rock plan, preliminary results indicate that parents respond with enthusiasm to the possibility of choice. This is just another way of saying that Alum Rock refutes one of the major assertions of those persons, especially school administrators, who oppose the voucher idea: that parents really don't want choices in schooling; that if given choices, they won't take advantage of them; and that, even if they take advantage of them, they will choose badly or will choose on the basis of class or race. Alum Rock demonstrates that parents are not as stupid or bigoted as educators think. It demonstrates that they want some freedom of choice in education and are perfectly capable of making wise decisions.

Two other voucher experiments are in prospect, one in East Hartford and one a statewide, or at least a multidistrict, plan in New Hampshire. Both are financed by the National Institute of Education, a division of the Office of Education. Although regulated, both will operate with fewer restrictions than Alum Rock and will therefore be a better test of the voucher idea. Both will allow the basic voucher to be supplemented by additional charges. Both will allow the participation of private nonreligious schools, and both would welcome parochial schools if the constitutional problem could be solved, but don't intend to fight that particular battle. Again, these experiments may do little to alleviate the financial plight of parochial schools, but they will speak to the related question of how parents would respond if they had a range of choice as to how their children should be educated.

Unhappily, it will be several more years before the lessons from East Hartford and New Hampshire can be illuminated for both educators and laypersons. Meanwhile the legislatures of some states, such as California and Connecticut, are facing court rulings that require them to produce statewide plans for financing their public schools on some kind of equalized basis acceptable to the court. A statewide voucher system would *seem* to be an ideal, tailormade solution to the "equal protection" problem—a problem likely to confront many more states in the near future. But supporting evidence from East Hartford and New Hampshire may come too late to be of any help.

Other experiments apart from vouchers will also throw some light on the same questions of parental choice. In a few cities, notably Pasadena, Berkeley, and Minneapolis, a limited number of parents can now choose one or more schools within the public system that have developed distinctive educational programs different from one another or from the rest of the public schools in the district. Again, preliminary results are encouraging, but it is too early for a definitive answer.

It is, of course, possible that the results of West's plan would be purely economic, not educational. If his plan were adopted, Catholic and non-Catholic parents using parochial schools would stop paying twice, but the kind and quality of education might remain more or less the same. After all, the quality of education in parochial schools has been dropping over the last decade as a consequence of the inflationary squeeze. West's plan might make it possible for them to raise tuition and improve quality, but the improvement might be marginal at best. The main advantage of his plan might simply be to provide parents with a choice of schools on geographic or religious grounds, with the quality of education remaining about where it is.

Also, the willingness of non-Catholics to have public money channeled to parochial schools in order to prevent those students from burdening the public system would presumably diminish as any type of voucher or per-capita payment approached the cost of public education. People might reason that such students might as well be in the public schools, since the cost is roughly the same, or that parochial schools might as well be converted to public. In this case the principal rationale for a pluralistic system might have to shift from salvaging the parochial schools, out of the enlightened self-interest of non-Catholics, to that of providing *all* parents with freedom to choose the kind of education they want.

Certainly that rationale has the broader appeal, and I, for one, would rather West put it at the center of his model than at the periphery. If his model were then adopted—if somehow its political and religious enemies, whose names are legion, could be brought around—I believe we would see a real diversity developing in primary and secondary schooling. Some schools would remain what they are now as far as teaching and the curriculum are concerned. Many others would change in an effort to attract a particular kind of parent. Any many new private schools would very probably come into being to do the same thing. For the first time we would have a truly pluralistic school system. For the first time the free market would have a chance to prove that a monopolistic state system, whose schools look and act alike from one end of the country to the other, is not really what the public wants.

Response to Koerner: Parochial School Survival—The Immediate Concern

E.G. West

Koerner would rather that I had placed the goal of universal free choice at the center of my model. Meanwhile he believes that my present proposal will face a legion of political and religious enemies. In my judgment his more radical policy of pushing for immediate and universal choice and competition will face the fullest opposition, and so much so that it is utopian to expect any lasting results from such a course. My proposal is far more modest than Koerner seems to realize. It is designed to offer advantages to all the participants—"to all the enemies." It will help the mass of public school users insofar as it prevents the inundation of their schools by refugees from bankrupt parochial schools. It will help the latter by enabling them to survive in periods of severe cost increase. It will meet, in my judgment and in that of lawyer Sugarman in this book, the objections of current members of the Supreme Court. My main proposal to introduce user taxes that contribute to future *increases* in the costs of education will not immediately unleash some universal frenzy of school switching. The relative advantages and disadvantages between the public and parochial schools will, in the near future, remain almost the same as at present. My main proposal only holds out some promise that the present parochial schools will not vanish but will survive in their present numbers.

It is significant, nevertheless, that as time goes on and as costs increase so strongly that the user taxes figure as an increasing proportion of total costs, the opportunity cost of withdrawing a child from the public system and transferring him/her to a private school will gradually fall. This may well begin to expand family choices when incomes rise, if we assume, as we usually do, that there is a high income elasticity of demand for education. But this will be a gradual process. The possibility of the proportion of public schools in the total supply declining will depend on their ability to meet any new competition. But certainly Koerner is right to intimate that, *in the long run*, the goals of pluralism, choice, competition, and increased efficiency are all more likely to be pursued. Koerner's almost urgent need to know now "what it will be like" when such a world is attained echos to some extent the popular fear against *sudden* change. One advantage of my proposal is that the change will not be sudden, yet in a few years we *can* expect some steady growth of choice.

Such gradual change will provide more meaningful experiments than those of the present voucher schemes that Koerner mentions. I believe that these schemes have failed in their objective of reinstating choice. If choice is to mean anything, it should mean choice among *all* the alternatives. The significant point about the Alum Rock and New Hampshire voucher experiments is that one major alternative—the parochial schools, which provide almost the only significant private alternative—has been ruled out on legal advice. Indeed it is these kinds of reasons that I started my original essay. Voucher schemes under the present constitutional setup have produced little more than "paper choice." I consider that the chances of legitimate choice ever being returned to American education waits upon the successful resolution of the problem of the "roadblock" of the First Amendment. Another necessary condition is the abolition of so-called free education and the reintroduction of positive prices, however modest in the first instance.

The Philosophical and Historical Interpretation of the First Amendment

E.G. West

Two contributors, Freeman and Coons, have urged (and I agree with them) that we return seriously to the original purposes of the First Amendment as seen through the eyes of the founding fathers. The present Court seems instead to be attached to its own rather different interpretation. It is their apparent intransigence on this issue that led me to avoid it in my opening essay. In searching for alternative approaches to solving the problem of satisfying the expressed political wishes of the New York State legislature with regard to parochial schools in that state, my assumption was that we could not hope for any immediate shifting of the Court's viewpoint. It is certainly a part of the issue that constantly needs to be kept alive, for who knows, one day a new Court *may* be amenable to new (or rather the old) reasoning. Readers who are newcomers to the problem will in any case welcome some aquaintance with these aspects.

I agree with Coon's interpretation of the founding fathers that the purpose of the First Amendment was simply that no orthodoxy be given official approval and that the ideal polity should contain, in Coon's words, "an unrestrained competition of ideas." I shall present here a picture of the historical circumstances surrounding the original legislation.

Madison, one of its authors, wrote the *Memorial and Remonstrance* in 1785 to protest against an act called the "Parsons Cause" that was then being advocated by Patrick Henry and other leaders in Virginia. It would have had the effect of establishing Christianity as the state religion. Madison asked: "Who does not see that the same authority which can establish Christianity in exclusion of other religions, may establish with the same ease any particular sect of Christians, in exclusion of all other sects." The temper of the times was becoming opposed to established religions, that is, situations in which government acknowledgment was given to one church with a consequent discrimination against other churches. Religious establishment was typical of European society, and the habit of it had been brought to America by some of the first colonists. Its dangers were being increasingly appreciated in a land being made up of many diverse people and cultures. Whereas before 1789 nine colonies had established churches (three Congregational and six Anglican), only five states still had them by the time the Constitution was adopted. In 1833 the Congregational Church was disestablished in Massachusetts, and church-state relations at last came to an end.

It was not only in the American colonies that establishment was coming under criticism. The British intellectual scene was alive with radical dissent. Philosophers such as David Hume and political economists such as Turgot in France and Adam Smith in Scotland were openly hostile to it. It will be useful indeed to quote some of Adam Smith's views in particular since his work *The Wealth of Nations* (published in 1776) was known to several of the founding fathers. (John Adam for example is known to have been an especially close reader of Smith's *Wealth of Nations*.) Smith explicitly looked toward the New World to produce that kind of new constitution that would avoid the errors of the old. The celebrated champion of the virtues of competition, with his new arguments he audaciously penetrated this very area of religious education; but the analysis here was a little more sophisticated. Teachers who depended for their living upon the fees of their pupils, Smith's argument began, were likely to be zealous and industrious. In contrast, those teachers who enjoyed payment from some other fund—such as a tithe, a land tax, an established salary, or a stipend—were more prone to giving themselves up to indolence. Established church systems resulted in this very outcome. They gave their teachers financial support independent of their "customers" the students; as a result, they subsequently became lazy and inefficient. This weakness led them to be complacent even in defending their own doctrines against the attacks of new religions and new teachers whose income *was* dependent upon their immediate customers—their "common people" listeners.

In this respect the teachers of new religions always had a considerable advantage in attacking those ancient and established systems of which the clergy, reposing themselves upon their benefices, had neglected to keep up the fervour of faith and devotion in the great body of people; and having given themselves up to indolence, were become altogether incapable of making any vigorous exertion in defence even of their own establishment.[1]

It may be asked whether, after all, the problem of monopoly religion would thus eventually solve itself. Unfortunately, Adam Smith argued, this was not so. The gradual encroachment of new religions subsequently forced the established one into vicious overreaction. The established clergy would eventually call upon the civil magistrate to persecute, destroy, or drive out their adversaries.

It was thus that the Roman Catholic clergy called upon the civil magistrate to persecute the protestants; and the Church of England, to persecute the dissenters; and that in general every religious sect, when it has once enjoyed for a century or two the security of a legal establishment, has found itself incapable of making any vigorous defence against any new sect which chose to attack its doctrine or discipline.[2]

Times of violent religious controversy were often times of equally violent political faction. Each political party allied itself with someone or other of the contending religious sects. The sect that supported the winning political party would then want some share in the spoils of office. "Their first demand was generally, that he [the civil magistrate] should silence and subdue all their adversaries; and their second, that he should bestow an independent provision on themselves. As they had generally contributed a good deal of the victory, it seemed not unreasonable that they should have some share in the spoil."[3] If politics had never called in the aid of religion, and never adopted the tenets of one sect more than those of another, Smith insisted, it would probably have dealt equally and impartially with all the different sects. Every person would have been able to choose his/her own priest and religion as he/she thought proper. But then comes a further shrewd and characteristic Smithian prediction. In the belief that it has very special reference to the present parochial school debate and historical environment in which the First Amendment was passed, I shall quote it here in full.

There would in this case, no doubt, have been a great multitude of religious sects. Almost every different congregation might probably have made a little sect by itself or have entertained some peculiar tenets of its own. Each teacher would no doubt have felt himself under the necessity of making the utmost exertion, and of using every art both to preserve and to increase the number of his disciples. But as every other teacher would have felt himself the same necessity, the success of no one teacher, or sect of teachers, could have been very great. The interested and active zeal of religious teachers can be dangerous and troublesome only where there is, either but one sect tolerated in the society, or where the whole of a large society is divided into two or three great sects; the teachers of each acting by concert under a regular discipline and subordination. But that zeal must be altogether innocent where the society is divided into two or three hundred, or perhaps into as many thousand small sects, of which no one could be considerable enough to disturb the public tranquility. The teachers of each sect, seeing themselves surrounded on all sides with more adversaries than friends, would be obliged to learn that candor and moderation which is so seldom to be found among the teachers of those great sects, whose tenets, being supported by the civil magistrate, are held in veneration by almost all the inhabitants of extensive kingdoms and empires, and who therefore see nothing round them but followers, disciples, and humble admirers.[4]

If the plan had been adopted of no ecclesiastical government, a plan put forward by the Independents in England toward the end of the English civil war, it would, argued Smith, have produced "the most philosophical good temper and moderation with regard to every sort of religious principle." He quoted the case of Pennsylvania where this happy result had occurred because "the law in reality favours no one sect more than another." And this resulted even though the Quakers happened to be in the majority. Provided, then, that the sects were sufficiently numerous, excessive zeal could not lead to much harm. On the contrary, there could be several good consequences. Smith believed that membership of little religious sects, especially in the towns, was conducive to successful civilization: "In little religious sects, accordingly, the morals of common people have been almost always remarkably regular and orderly; *generally much more so than in the established church.*"[5]

Adam Smith concluded his chapter with the observation that the expense of the institutions for education and religious instruction is beneficial to the whole society. But rather than supporting it by the general contribution of the whole society, the government could usually leave it to be financed by individual beneficiaries. "This expense, however, might perhaps with equal propriety, and even for some advantage, be defrayed altogether by those who receive the immediate benefit of such education and instruction, or, by the voluntary contribution of those who think they have occasion for either the one or the other.[6] In the terms of modern economics, Adam Smith saw external benefits arising from religious education; the benefits, however, were positive *on the average*; the *marginal* external benefits were probably zero. But all this depended on a wide diffusion of religions, or as Smith might even say, a "free market in religions." The external, or public, benefits from such diffused religious instruction would *not* be generated, however, if the government sponsored its own favored religious instruction. The external benefits would be even more difficult to internalize if the public instructors were financed from taxes upon the clients of private instructors. Referring to public teachers, Smith complained:

Their salaries too put the private teacher, who would pretend to come into competition with them, in the same with a merchant who attempts to trade without a bounty, in competition with those who trade with a considerable one. If he sells his goods at nearly the same price, he cannot have the same profit, and poverty and beggary at least, if not bankruptcy and ruin, will infallibly be his lot.[7]

In my opinion, it is not too fanciful to believe that the kind of world that the founding fathers were seeking was similar to this one of "a free market in religion" that Smith advocated. It is this kind of world that provides for what Coons describes as "an unrestrained competition of ideas." And such a world cannot thrive where there is a system of secular public education, provided at common schools, free of charge yet financed from a common fund to which everybody contributes tax revenues.

In opposing *established* religions it should not be assumed that the founding fathers were not basically religious people. Many of them were in fact deeply religious although uncommitted to a particular church. Religious belief includes the theistic and the nontheistic. The Deists and nondeistic believers during the late eighteenth century were fundamentally religious people. Everybody's need was for a constitution that would allow people to enjoy the pursuit of religious experience and thought in *all* its manifestations. In my opinion it is a mistake to imagine that the First

Amendment established such a "wall of separation" between church and state that it attempted a divorce of religion from the social and political realities of life.[8] One would not speak of a "wall of separation" between the state and freedom of speech, press and assembly. Freedom of religion was seen in the same light as these other freedoms when the Constitution was written. The First Amendment was aimed merely at prohibiting the federal government from establishing a religion and at established guarantees for the free exercise of religion to all.

It is probably impossible for any education to be religiously neutral. First, there is the strong possibility that children will not have the chance to become acquainted with religion because it is "crowded out" by secular or scientific subjects. Second, secularism itself might give rise to a more coherent school of thought, ideology, or movement. In this sense, some people would strongly fear that the religion of secular humanism is being represented, if not inculcated, in the modern-day public school, despite its attempts at neutrality. "Humanism is a faith in the people, in all humanity, and its science has a means of obtaining truth. There is also a quest for the ethical and spiritual values of life through philosophy, science, the arts and literature."[9] The essential part of the humanist creed is that life must be viewed of the purely natural, "reasonable" level; and it is this disposition which leads them to their views on such things as abortion, sexual freedom, euthanasia, and divorce. Bearing in mind that the founding fathers' concept of religious freedom emphasized the right *not* to believe in one particular religion, the question now is whether this right is being respected when the religion of secular humanism abounds in public schools. In *Dorcaso v. Watkins* (1952) Justice Black observed:

We repeat and again reaffirm that neither a State nor the Federal Government can constitutionally force a person "to profess his belief or disbelief" in any religion. Neither can constitutionally pass laws or impose requirements which aid all religions as against unbelievers and neither can aid those religions based on the belief in the existence of God as against those religions founded on different beliefs.[10]

Justice Black's comments were accompanied by the following footnote: "Among the religions in this country which do not teach what would commonly be considered a belief in the existence of God are Buddhism, Taoism, Ethical Culture, Secular Humanism, and others." Clearly the Supreme Court has formalized the right of nontheistic religions to exist and to enjoy the protections of the Constitution; but does it not go beyond protection when some of these religions are provided, in public schools, free of charge, and others have to help finance them?

One cannot complain that indoctrination, or value inculcation, occurs in schools, for, as Coons observes, this is the lot of all involuntary students, public and private. One must then endorse his verdict that: "The problem is compulsion; for all but the rich, public school is an inescapable official philosophy . . . [and this] is a reproach to the values that inform the First

Amendment." Coons also expresses the hope that the Court will become wary of "ideological monoliths irrespective of their secular, religious, or humanistic credentials." Given a more balanced sensitivity, "the Court might perceive anti-Establishment—even Jeffersonian—virtues in such laws as it has latterly slaughtered."

The Supreme Court, however, did once openly frustrate the notion that, in the name of consensus, public school experience must be universal. As Coons reminds us, this was in the case of *Pierce v. The Society of Sisters*. The judgment here upheld the right of parents to choose private schools instead of public schools where they felt it necessary. Subsequently, however, the Court's verdict was itself atrophied; and this by what Coons calls "public economics." But public economics is not an external or supernatural force; it is the outcome of political decisions, especially about the way in which public schools are financed and the way in which the taxes that supplies them with resources are collected, an outcome that is inimical since their clientele are made to pay twice. One may try to defend the Court with the argument that it was powerless to challenge these decisions on public economics because they concerned the sacred territory of government within its own respective sphere under the separation of powers? If so, however, the Supreme Court will be similarly powerless to challenge any further modifications in public economics relating to the mix of public taxes and public finance of education, modifications such as those in my proposals? Coons seems to believe these (user tax) proposals would incur close judicial scrutiny. If so, there seems to be yet another asymmetry in the Court's approach.

Finally, on historical aspects, I would like to draw attention to one irony with respect to the influence of Horace Mann, the person who has come to be known as "the father of our public schools." It is often forgotten that although Mann argued for nonsectarian schooling, he did not want an irreligious education.[11] He especially advocated character education; and this could not be effective, he insisted, unless the child were introduced to Christian religion. Mann's common school sought to bring about not only a "publically financed and free" schooling, but a schooling wherein ethical character was developed and spiritual needs satisfied with the help of the Bible—but used in a nonsectarian manner, that is, without comment. In his celebrated Fourth of July Oration in Boston (1842), he observed:

I have said that schools should have been established for the education of the whole people. These schools should have been of a more perfect character than any which have ever yet existed. . . . In them the principles of morality should have been copiously intermingled with the principles of science. . . . The lives of great and good men should have been help up for admiration and example, and especially the life and character of Jesus Christ, as the sublimest pattern of benevolence, of purity, of self-sacrifice, ever exhibited to mortals.[12]

Recent Supreme Court interpretations of the First and Fourteenth Amendments have led it to do away with such preferential use of the Bible in public schools on the grounds of unconstitutionality (*Schempp v. The School District of Abington*, 1963 and *Chamberlain v. Dade County Board of Public Instruction*, 1964). The Supreme Court presumably believes that it has at last made public schools neutral. This is not so, for, as I have argued, the "established" and compulsory religion of the public schools seems to be that of secular humanism. But clearly the common school envisaged by Horace Mann failed the test of neutrality also, for, to repeat Madison's words, Mann's public authority would be "establishing Christianity in exclusion of other religions."

Those who today admire the ideals of religious education for which Horace Mann was striving, cannot to this extent support the present public system. Moreover, they can entertain little hope in the near future that the Horace Mann model will be reinstated, since the Supreme Court's recent judgments strongly preclude it. Their only hope is in the encouragement of those remaining schools where traditional religions are still taught, but the encouragement cannot take the form of "aid" directly from the public purse. The user tax system as explained in my proposal is one avenue that could begin to meet their wishes, and it takes the form of reducing "hostility" and *not* of providing "aid."

Notes

1. Adam Smith, *The Wealth of Nations*, Edwin Cannan edition, Methuen, London, 1950, Book 2, p. 273.

2. Ibid., p. 274.

3. Ibid., p. 277.

4. Ibid., p. 280.

5. Ibid., p. 301, my italics.

6. See Friedman's comment in this volume and my response to it.

7. Smith, op. cit., p. 265.

8. Brother D.P. Draney, *The First Amendment and Freedom of Religion in Education*, Catholic School Administrators Association of New York State, January 1975.

9. *The Humanist*, March 1962, quoted in Draney, ibid.

10. *Dorcaso v. Watkins*, (1952).

11. J.B. Kristensen, "The Common School of Horace Mann That Died in Infancy," *Education Freedom*, 9(1), Winter 1970-71; 26.

12. Horace Mann, quoted in Kristensen, ibid.

Index

About the Author

E.G. West received the Ph.D. in economics from London University and was a research fellow at the University of Chicago in 1966. He is professor of Economics at Carleton University in Ottawa and during the 1975-1976 academic year he is Visiting Professor at Virginia Polytechnic Institute and State University, Blacksburg. Dr. West is the author of *Education and the State* (1965); *Adam Smith: The Man and His Works* (1969); *Education and Industrial Revolution* (1975); and is a frequent contributor to economics journals.

Related Lexington Books

Berke, Joel S. and Kirst, Michael W., *Federal Aid to Education*, 384 pp., 1972

Cohn, Elchanan, *The Economics of State Aid to Education*, 192 pp., 1974

Davis, J. Ronnie and Morall, John F., *Evaluating Educational Invest-ments*, 144 pp., 1974

Levin, Betsy, *Future Directions for School Finance Reform*, 304 pp., 1975

Sullivan, Daniel J., *Public Aid to Nonpublic Schools*, 146 pp., 1974